W9-AFP-527

NIKOLAI I. BUKHARIN

HOOVER INSTITUTION BIBLIOGRAPHICAL SERIES

HOOVER INSTITUTION BIBLIOGRAPHICAL SERIES XXXVII

NIKOLAI I. BUKHARIN

A BIBLIOGRAPHY

With Annotations, Including the Locations of His Works in Major American and European Libraries

Compiled and Edited
by
SIDNEY HEITMAN

THE HOOVER INSTITUTION
ON WAR, REVOLUTION AND PEACE
STANFORD UNIVERSITY · STANFORD, CALIFORNIA
1969

The Hoover Institution on War, Revolution and Peace, founded at Stanford University in 1919 by the late President Herbert Hoover, is a center for advanced study and research on public and international affairs in the twentieth century. The views expressed in its publications are entirely those of the authors and do not necessarily reflect the views of the Hoover Institution.

Library of Congress Catalog Card Number: 68-28101
Printed in West Germany
by Fremdsprachendruckerei Dr. Peter Belej, München 13

CONTENTS

PREFACE

There is an old anecdote about the Russian who, when asked by an immigration inspector at the French border to name his profession, replied, "*Je suis intelligent.*" In pre-Revolutionary Russia to be a member of the intelligentsia was profession enough. And such was the role of Nikolai I. Bukharin, one of the foremost intellectual leaders in the Bolshevik Party during the decades preceding and following the 1917 Russian Revolution. Lenin evaluated him as the Party's "most notable and eminent theoretician." The "October" generation regarded Bukharin as a "theoretical Hercules."

If Marx and Engels had provided their followers with the broad philosophical rationale and the general plans for the coming world revolution, their ambiguous legacy posed many problems for those who, like the Bolsheviks, were determined to translate theory into action. It was Bukharin who undertook the enormous task of transforming classical Marxist doctrine into an operative instrument of revolutionary action by rectifying certain of its logical defects, accounting for the failure of some of its crucial predictions, and applying it to every phase of socialist life. Thus it can be said that Bukharin's greatest achievement was the accommodation of Marxism to twentieth-century developments.

Bukharin was born of school teacher parents in Moscow in 1888. He was educated at the University of Moscow and joined the Russian Social Democratic Workers' Party in 1906, the same year he published in a student newspaper his first serious study on the theory of national economic development. As the result of his Marxist agitation he was in prison or in exile from 1909 to 1911. In 1912, after he had fled Russia, he met Lenin in Cracow, and their historic personal and professional relationship began. In 1916 he went to New York, where he co-edited with Trotsky an émigré socialist newspaper, *Novyi Mir*, and helped to organize the nucleus of what was to become the American Communist Party.

Following the March Revolution, Bukharin returned to Moscow, where he assumed leadership of the organization that won Moscow for the Bolshevik Party. Later, and until his decline instigated by Stalin in 1929, he attained some of the highest posts in the Russian and international communist hierarchy, including the presidency of the Comintern in 1926. Bukharin's most enduring influence on the development of Bolshevism, however, resulted not from his manipulations of the symbols or instruments of power, but from the force of his thought. In some of his major works, Lenin expressed theories for which he received sole credit, although they were originally articulated by Bukharin.

Lenin's classic treatise, "State and Revolution" [1] contains many of the ideas expressed a year earlier in Bukharin's "Theory of the Imperialist State" (see entry No. 583). Many of Bukharin's theories for twentieth-century Marxism, whether derived directly from him or indirectly through Lenin, have since been incorporated into standard communist doctrine. One of Bukharin's most widely read books, "The Economics of the Transition Period" (see entry No. 288), provides a comprehensive theory of the actual process by which capitalism is transferred into communism following a proletarian seizure of power. Today, there are indications that factions in some of the East European satellite countries are being guided by theories expounded in this work in determining current economic policies, although none have gone so far as to name Bukharin as the source. Any such acknowledgment to Bukharin no doubt will have to await Bukharin's complete rehabilitation from his fall from grace during the Stalin period, and that may be long in coming.

Bukharin was a favorite of Lenin, and many believed that he would inherit Lenin's mantle after the latter's death. Stalin, however, with his greater organizational skills and pragmatic approach, was able to outmaneuver Bukharin, the intellectual, in the political arena. As one who would brook no opposition, Stalin found intolerable Bukharin's strong advocacy of Lenin's New Economic Policy in preference to his own First Five-Year Plan. Yet before he launched Bukharin's official downgrading, Stalin took advantage of Bukharin's prestige by using him as an ally in his political struggle against Trotsky and Zinoviev. After 1929, Bukharin's official influence steadily waned, until eventually, in 1938, he was tried and executed for treason in the last of the infamous purge trials.

In 1962, as a result of the somewhat liberalized political climate of the post-Stalin period, Bukharin was partially rehabilitated in the Soviet Union, although his views were still considered heretical. A more thorough rehabilitation seemed to be indicated by a 1965 report that one of Bukharin's best known works, his "A B C of Communism" (see entry No. 194), would be republished in the U.S.S.R. for the first time since its suppression in 1938, but until now it has not appeared.

Regardless of his present official status, it is evident that Bukharin's brief but consequential career left an indelible imprint on Bolshevism. At the height of his career, he was considered by Soviet and non-Soviet contemporaries as a highly creative, original contributor not only to Marxism but to twentieth-century thought generally. Fortunately, in spite of Stalinist suppression, most of his published writings are available to scholars in the West. In addition to his major works, some of which were mentioned earlier, Bukharin wrote literally hundreds of newspaper and periodical articles, editorials, and popular tracts, as well as scores of public speeches which helped to shape and articulate the views of the Communist Party on a multitude of contemporary problems.

---

[1] *Gosudarstvo i revoliutsiia, uchenie marksizma o gosudarstve i zadachi proletariata v revoliutsii* (1917).

Because of a renewed interest and need for further exploration of Bukharin's impact on applied communism, the Hoover Institution plans the publication of two additional works about Bukharin—one a political biography and the other a study of his theory of revolution. Both of these works are being written by Professor Sidney Heitman, a leading Bukharin specialist, to whom the Hoover Institution is also indebted for the compilation of this first complete and authoritative bibliography of those works of Bukharin which can be found in the major American and European libraries. With this bibliography, a handy tool is now available for the intensive study of Bukharin's role as a major contributor to modern Marxist thought, one of the basic forces affecting our times. Students of world communism are sure to find this compilation a welcome help in their research; scholars concerned mainly with the history and development of communist thought will find it an indispensable guide.

K. Maichel, Curator
East European Collection
The Hoover Institution on War, Revolution and Peace

INTRODUCTION

Background

There has long been a need for a comprehensive guide to the works of Nikolai Bukharin, despite the appearance several years ago of two bibliographies intended to fill what was then a complete gap in this important area of Soviet studies. In 1958 the writer published a basic checklist of titles in *An Annotated Bibliography of Nikolai I. Bukharin's Published Works* (Fort Collins, Colo., 1958) which represented the first effort ever to catalog Bukharin's voluminous writings and published statements. This limited edition of 200 copies, privately printed and quickly exhausted, was followed the next year by a revised and enlarged edition combining the writer's work with that of Dr. Peter Knirsch, who had been conducting research on Bukharin independently at the East European Institute of the Free University of Berlin. Under Dr. Knirsch's direction, *N. I. Bucharin*, Vol. I in the *Bibliographische Mitteilungen des Osteuropa-Instituts an der Freien Universität Berlin* (Berlin, 1959), was compiled and issued. The original list of some 500 titles in the early version was augmented and expanded by additional publication data in the second edition.

Although these two pioneering efforts served their intended purpose of filling an important and conspicuous gap in the available basic Soviet reference works, both were flawed by certain unavoidable shortcomings. It became increasingly apparent that a final, authoritative compilation was needed. The impetus that led to the preparation of the present edition came from two sources. In 1963 the compiler was commissioned by Mr. Clemens Heller of the École Pratique des Hautes Études in Paris to edit a comprehensive list of Bukharin's works as a guide for its planned reproduction of his published writings and speeches in microform. The following year, Mr. Karol Maichel, on behalf of the Hoover Institution on War, Revolution and Peace, Stanford University, arranged for the independent publication of the bibliography in the Institution's Bibliographical Series.

The features that distinguish this edition from the earlier efforts are several. First, while it is based upon and integrates the content of the two previous volumes, this volume adds considerably to both with the inclusion of titles discovered since their publication; second, it rectifies errors, gaps, and inconsistencies contained in the preceding compilations and generally provides more detailed and complete publication data for each item than was originally intended or possible in the earlier versions. Thus it provides a complete bibliographical "history," to the extent that this can be known of each of Bukharin's individual works, including such information as the original titles under which his writings were published, variations in these titles in subsequent editions, and complete data for all translations and modified versions of these works, together with annotations and indications of the locations of each entry, when known. Finally, the entries are presented here in chronological order by year, with a comprehensive system of cross-referencing and a complete alphabetical index.

All modifications are intended to make this definitive edition more useful and serviceable than either of its predecessors as a basic reference tool.

Arrangement of Entries

The arrangement of entries is basically chronological, according to the *year of original publication* of each of Bukharin's works, beginning with 1906-1910, the approximate time of his first known publication, and ending with 1963, the year of the last known republication of one of his works. Within each yearly division the entries are listed *alphabetically,* since it is not possible to determine the precise time of publication—or writing—of many of his individual works, thereby precluding chronological presentation within the annual sections.

While *main entries* are listed according to year of original publication (with a few necessary exceptions to be noted further on) followed by a complete bibliographical "history" of all subsequent editions, versions, and translations of a main work, *cross-reference entries* indicate the year of writing or other production of a main work when the date of production and the date of original publication differ. Cross-reference entries also indicate under the appropriate year each subsequent edition, version, or translation of works in main entries. These are usually identified by a short title with a reference back to the number of the main entry. Thus entries under a particular year provide a comprehensive list of titles of works by Bukharin or of works produced during that year in which his writings or published statements appeared, whether as original publications or in some type of re-issue. Hopefully, it will now be readily possible for the user to determine the scope and character of Bukharin's literary production for any calandar year during his career and of such re-issues of his works as were published after his death in 1938.

Each main entry includes complete publication data for the original publication and all subsequent versions insofar as can be ascertained. Cross-references under the appropriate year of re-issue or translation of items in main entries refer the user back to the main entry for complete bibliographical data.

In regard to the order of listing titles, no distinction is made among types of publications—articles, books, documents, or published speeches. Each entry is listed by title, followed either by the publication data, in the case of independent publications, or by an indication of the publication (journal, newspaper, symposium, etc.) in which the item appeared. Generally, in listing subsequent editions, versions, and re-issues of a particular work, Russian editions are given in chronological order, followed by non-Russian translations, first into other Slavic languages and then into non-Slavic languages. Where Bukharin's works appeared first—or only—in a non-Russian language, the entry is listed by the non-Russian title, followed by data pertaining to subsequent issues of the work. While certain departures from these general rules of entry were necessary because of the unique character of some items, in all instances the intent is to make each entry as consistent, logical and self-explanatory as possible.

System of Alphabetization

The system of alphabetization within yearly divisions (and in the index) is based on the Latin alphabet. Latin characters in non-Cyrillic titles are listed according to the normal rules of alphabetization. Cyrillic titles are listed alphabetically in accordance with their *English transliterated equivalents,* based on the Library of Congress system of transliteration, minus diacritical marks*. Awkward though this arrangement may at first appear, it provides an arbitrary consistency and a common denominator for an alphabetical listing of all entries in the chronological sections of the bibliography and in the index not possible with any of the alternative listing schemes considered before the adoption of this method. Considering the many languages in which Bukharin's works were published, the absence of standard or universally employed methods of listing Cyrillic together with non-Cyrillic materials, and the differences in systems of transliteration, no other conceivable procedure offered so many advantages where the interests of consistency and clarity were concerned.

An alphabetical index at the end of the bibliography lists titles of all original works and subsequent issues, each followed by the main entry number. Thus it is possible to locate items when a title, but not the year of publication, is known. The system of alphabetization in the index, as indicated, follows the rules for alphabetization within yearly divisions.

Form and Content of Entries

The form of entry used here is based generally upon the style recommended by Blanche P. McCrum and Helen D. Jones, *Bibliographical Procedures and Styles; A Manual for Bibliographers in the Library of Congress* (Washington, The Library of Congress; General Reference and Bibliography Division, 1954). Owing to certain peculiarities of Soviet publication practices and to the distinctive nature of some of the material included in this bibliography, it has been necessary to modify and adapt the recommendations of the manual in order to achieve the intended aim here of providing a guide to the known works of Bukharin in their various editions and versions and to their character and locations in major Western libraries. Further complicating the effort to follow the Library of Congress style and to achieve uniformity and consistency is the fact that the bibliography includes material published in seventeen languages—Russian, Byelorussian, Ukrainian, Polish, Czech, Lithuanian, Latvian, Finnish, French, German, English, Italian, Spanish, Magyar, Swedish, Norwegian, and Japanese— a reflection of the wide range of Communist activities and of Bukharin's importance in the international Communist movement. In the effort to standardize entries and to minimize distracting adaptations of multi-lingual titles, the entries are listed in the alphabet of each language in which Bukharin's works appeared—Cyrillic and Latin respectively (with the exception of one transliterated Japanese title)—with as close adherence to the Library of Congress bibliographical style as is practical. While places of publication and pubulishers are similarly given in the original language and alphabet, collation, annotations, cross-references, and various bibliographical symbols employ English, with

* Titles with numerals preceding the initial word are listed in *numerical order before all other titles* because of the multiplicity of languages involved.

American usage as to general style and the recommendations of the Library of Congress Manual as to general form.

Entries consist of six types of publications: (a) independent publications authored or co-authored by Bukharin, such as books or pamphlets; (b) articles or essays in symposia or other book-form publications; (c) articles published in newspapers and periodicals; (d) documents; (e) speeches or remarks made to various meetings and organizations published either in their protocols or as separate publications; and (f) miscellaneous material, such as introductions or prefaces to the works of other authors. Notably lacking are references to unpublished material—with one or two exceptions—such as manuscripts, personal papers and records, correspondence, and memoirs or notes, which do not exist so far as is known outside the Soviet Union and which, if they exist there, are inaccessible to Western scholars.

Within each entry, the following information, to the extent known,* is listed in the order indicated:

(a) Independent publications: (1) full title; (2) co-authors, where appropriate; (3) place of publication; (4) publisher; (5) date of publication; (6) collation; (7) location of the item indicated by special library symbols.
(b) Articles and essays in collections: (1) title of article or essay; (2) title of publication in which it appeared; then as (3) through (7) above.
(c) Articles in newspapers and periodicals: (1) title of the article; (2) title of the newspaper or periodical in which it appeared; (3) volume, number, date, etc. of issue in which article appeared; (4) pages of issue in which article appeared. Locations of newspapers and periodicals are given in a composite list of "Periodicals and Newpapers Cited" at the beginning of the bibliography but not after each periodical or newspaper entry, in order to avoid unnecessary repetition.
(d) Documents: entries vary in accordance with the nature of the document and the information available.
(e) Speeches: precise or approximate titles (the latter enclosed in brackets), followed by the publication in which they appear in accordance with either (a) or (c) above.
(f) Miscellaneous material: entries vary in accordance with the nature of the material and the information available.

This order of information within entries applies to *main entries*, which are listed under the year of initial *publication* of each title, regardless of whether the date of writing or of other production differs from the publication date (with a few exceptions deemed necessary so as not to create complications and confusion). Cross-reference entries are discussed in the following section.

Annotations, Cross-References and Location Symbols

Although no effort was made to analyze the content or historical circumstances surrounding every item listed, random annotations intended to render the bibliography more useful have been made. In some instances these clarify the nature or content of an entry; in others, they date the time of writing or of publication more precisely than is indicated in the standard entry form; otherwise they furnish information discovered by the compiler appropriate to the more effective use of the guide.

A comprehensive system of cross-referencing, consisting of titles only, indicates the year in which a work was originally produced where this differs from the date of actual publication; also listed are all subsequent editions and ver-

---

* See section on "Missing Data."

sions following the original publication of an item, which will be found under the appropriate subsequent years. Other cross-reference entries provide the titles of articles and essays in collected works or symposia under the year of original writing or publication. Here again, in the instance of cross-references, minor departures from the general rules have been made occasionally in the interest of clarity.

When the main entries and cross-references were compiled, the entire chronological bibliography was numbered consecutively; where entries had to be inserted after the numbering, sub-numbers *(e. g., 257, 257a,* 258) were inserted so as not to disrupt numerical continuity or the alphabetical order of entries within each yearly division.

Among the departures from the Library of Congress Manual is the inclusion in each entry of symbols indicating the locations of the items listed when this information is appropriate and known. These symbols represent the holdings of 41 major libraries possessing Soviet collections located in the West, and they were devised by combining standard union catalog library symbols with invented symbols where standard designations were lacking. The libraries and their symbols appearing in the bibliography are listed at the beginning of the chronological section.

No effort was made to survey the holdings of every library possessing one or more copies of Bukharin's works, and undoubtedly some important collections have been omitted. Neither was it possible for obvious reasons to determine the holdings of libraries in the Soviet Union or in Communist-bloc countries. Despite the omissions, however, enough locations are indicated to enable researchers to obtain copies or reproductions of Bukharin's works in all the major Western countries, and considering the revolution in library science and in printing and reprinting technology in recent years, as well as the rapid expansion of Soviet collections in numerous research and university libraries, any listing of libraries holding Bukharin's works would become obsolete as soon as it was compiled. In a few instances, the notation "available in various libraries" was added in place of listing specific libraries, where the corresponding publication is widely distributed. In other instances, where items could not be located in the West, the absence of a location symbol or the notation "contents and location unknown" indicates the lack of this information.

In order to eliminate repetition in the numerous citations of newpapers and periodicals in which Bukharin's works appeared, publication data and location are given in a composite list of periodicals and newspapers cited at the beginning of the bibliography.

Missing Data

The information contained in this bibliography has been compiled over many years from a variety of standard and in some instances unorthodox sources. Standard bibliographies proved to be of relatively little value, inasmuch as never before has there been a systematic compilation of Bukharin's works.

Many of them were produced clandestinely and therefore escaped the notice of various national and union catalogs, and others of his works fall outside the scope of existing bibliographical tools. The card files of various libraries provided rich sources of information; the printed catalog of the Russian Foreign Historical Archive, formerly in Prague, furnished much valuable data, and various general, union, and specialized bibliographies proved to be of lesser value. Some references to Bukharin's works were uncovered in footnotes or bibliographies in his own works and in those of other writers, in advertisements appearing in Soviet newspapers, journals, and books, and in other similar "unorthodox" sources. Since *Pravda* and *Izvestiia* and several journals are not adequately indexed for the years of Bukharin's career, a page-by-page search had to be made for signed or attributed articles and accounts of his speeches. Many titles not formerly known to the compiler, as well as locations of Bukharin's works in German libraries, are included here as a result of the diligent efforts of Dr. Knirsch.

Although every reasonable and practical effort, up to and at times exceeding the point of diminishing returns, was made to compile and present complete data for every work produced by Bukharin and subsequently re-issued, gaps and omissions exist—some known and, undoubtedly, others unknown. Sometimes library index cards contained incomplete data; sometimes obscure references provided the only source of incomplete information; and at still other times dependence upon the bibliographical work of other compilers accounts for certain lapses of information. Where such gaps occur, they are indicated by standard symbols (n.p. for no place of publication or no publisher indicated or known; 192—? or 1922(?) where uncertainty as to dating exists; or [?] when pertinent information is lacking and cannot be determined) or "contents and location unknown" in instances of collections of articles authored or co-authored by Bukharin which could not be located and obtained for examination. In a number of entries, either the collation of books or the pages within a periodical on which Bukharin's work appeared are omitted when such information was not available or obtainable with reasonable effort. Most notably lacking are references to Bukharin's unpublished papers, as indicated above, and to unsigned editorials and articles in *Pravda, Izvestiia,* and other periodicals, which he undoubtedly published anonymously during the decade of the 1930's but which cannot now be identified. In general, whenever bibliographical data of one kind or another is lacking, this is indicated either by an approprate symbol or by a notation.

Throughout, then, despite certain departures from standard bibliographical forms and practices, the effort has been to render this bibliography as comprehensive, useful, and convenient as possible within the limits of the economics of printing and of the dictates of common sense.

ACKNOWLEDGEMENTS

Perhaps only those who have themselves attempted to compile an extensive bibliography can appreciate fully the enormous debt owed by the writer to a host of colleagues in the international fellowship of scholars. Special acknowledgement is due the following, however inadequate this token of gratitude may be: Mr. Clemens Heller of the École Pratique des Hautes Études; Mr. Melville J. Ruggles; Mr. Karol Maichel, Curator of the East European Collection of the Hoover Institution on War, Revolution and Peace; Dr. Peter Knirsch; Dr. J. Leo Cefkin; Dr. Robert M. Slusser; Dr. Marin Pundeff; Mr. J. G. Bell; Dr. Alexander Dallin; Dr. Henry L. Roberts; Dr. Kermit E. McKenzie; Dr. John E. Flaherty; and Professor Emeritus Geroid T. Robinson. An inexpressible debt is owed to the staffs of many libraries throughout the United States and Europe, and special thanks are owed to my colleagues at Colorado State University, Dean Austin O. Simonds and Professor George R. McMurray.

It is a pleasure also to acknowledge the debt owed the Social Science Research Council for financial support that made this volume possible, as well as the Ford Foundation, the Rockefeller Foundation, the Social Science Foundation of the University of Denver, and Colorado State University. Of special significance is the assistance rendered by Professor Philip E. Mosely of Columbia University, to whom the writer is privileged to express his profound appreciation.

Finally, to Frances R. Heitman goes an expression of thanks reserved by the academic community only for those long-suffering and indispensible persons who share fully the labors and anxieties of their husbands engaged in literary or scholarly effort, but who seldom receive more tangible recognition in the larger world than inadequate tributes such as this.

Sidney Heitman

Colorado State University
Fort Collins, Colorado

December 1968

LIST OF LIBRARIES AND SYMBOLS *

BDIC	Bibliothèque de Documentation Internationale Contemporaine et Musée de la Grande Guerre (Paris)
BHW	Bibliothek des Hamburgischen Weltwirtschafts-Archivs
BiN	Bibliothèque Nationale (Paris)
BIOG	Bibliothek des Instituts für osteuropäische Geschichte und Landeskunde an der Universität Tübingen
BIW	Bibliothek des Instituts für Weltwirtschaft an der Universität Kiel
BKH	Bibliothek der Kirchlichen Hochschule Berlin-Zehlendorf
BM-P	Bibliothek des Max-Planck-Instituts für ausländisches öffentliches Recht und Völkerrecht (Heidelberg)
BrM	British Museum (London)
BS	Bayerische Staatsbibliothek (Munich)
BSPD	Bibliothek der SPD (Landesverband Berlin)
CLSU	University of Southern California (Los Angeles)
CLU	University of California in Los Angeles
CSt-H	Hoover Institution on War, Revolution and Peace (Stanford)
CtY	Yale University (New Haven)
CU	University of California (Berkeley)
DLC	Library of Congress (Washington)
DS	Deutsche Staatsbibliothek (Berlin)
ICU	University of Chicago
IEUS	Institut zur Erforschung der UdSSR (Munich)
InI	International Institute for Social History (Amsterdam)
InU	Indiana University (Bloomington)
IU	University of Illinois (Urbana)

* These are arbitrary symbols designed for use in this bibliography in the absence of any standard, universally used international system of symbols.

MH Harvard University (Cambridge)

MiU University of Michigan (Ann Arbor)

NjP Princeton University

NN New York Public Library

NNC Columbia University (New York)

NNU New York University

NS-U Niedersächsische Staats- und Universitätsbibliothek (Göttingen)

OCl Cleveland Public Library

OFU-G Osteuropa-Institut an der Freien Universität Berlin, Abteilung für Osteuropäische Geschichte

OFU-R Osteuropa-Institut an der Freien Universität Berlin, Abteilung für Osteuropäisches Recht

OFU-S Osteuropa-Institut an der Freien Universität Berlin, Abteilung für Osteuropäische Soziologie

OFU-W Osteuropa-Institut an der Freien Universität Berlin, Abteilung für Osteuropäische Wirtschaft

RZIA Российский Заграничный Исторический Архив **

SB-N Stadtbücherei Berlin-Neukölln

SL Stadtbücherei Lübeck

UFU Universitätsbibliothek der Freien Universität Berlin

UL-H University Library (Helsinki)

WaU University of Washington (Seattle)

WB Westdeutsche Bibliothek (Marburg-Lahn)

** Formerly in Prague; removed to the Soviet Union after World War II.

LIST OF PERIODICALS AND NEWSPAPERS CITED

1. *Агитатор*. Kharkov, 1925—1932. *Location unknown*
2. *Die Arbeiterpolitik; Wochenschrift für wissenschaftlichen Sozialismus*. Bremen, 1916—1919. *Location unknown*
3. *Авангард*. Tula, 1925—1929. *Location unknown*
4. *Большевик; Политико-экономический двухнедельник ЦК ВКП(б)*. Moscow, 1921—. *Available in various libraries*
5. *The Class Struggle*. New York, 1917—1919; 1931—1937. *CSt-H*
6. *The Communist International*. London, New York, 1919—? *NN NNC CSt-H*
7. *The Communist Review*. London, 1921—1953. *CSt-H*
8. *Экономическая жизнь*. Moscow, 1918—? *NN CSt-H BS BIW*
9. *Экономический сборник*. Tula, 1921. *Location unknown*
10. *Еженедельник правды*. Moscow, 1919—1920. *Location unknown*
11. *Foreign Affairs*. New York, 1922—. *Available in various libraries*
12. *International Press Correspondence (Inprecor)*. Place of publication varies, 1921—. *NN NNC CSt-H*
13. *Die Internationale; eine Zeitschrift für Praxis und Theorie des Marxismus*. Berlin, 1915—1938. *CSt-H*
14. *Internationale Presse-Korrespondenz*. Berlin, Vienna, 1921—1935. *CSt-H*
15. *Историк марксист*. Moscow, 1926—1941. *CSt-H*
16. *Известия* (Центрального Исполнительного Комитета СССР . . .) Petrograd, Moscow, 1917—. *Available in various libraries*
17. *Известия*. Kazan, n. d. *Location unknown*
18. *Jugend-Internationale; Kampforgan der Kommunistischen Jugend-Internationale*. Zürich, Berlin, Vienna, 1915—1934. *CSt-H*
19. *Klassekampen; Organ for den Revolusjonaere Ungdom i Norge*. Oslo, 1908—? *Location unknown*

20. *Коммунист.* Petrograd, Moscow, 1918. *NN NNC CSt-H*

21. *Коммунист.* Geneva, 1915. *NNC CSt-H*

22. *Коммунист; Теоретический и политический журнал.* Moscow, n. d. *Location unknown*

23. *Коммунистический Интернационал.* Petrograd, Moscow, 1919—1943. *NNC CSt-H*

24. *Коммунистический путь.* Kazan, 1921—1925. *Location unknown*

25. *Die Kommunistische Internationale.* Berlin, Hamburg, 1919—1933. *NNC CSt-H BS UFU BIOG IEUS BSPD*

26. *Красная газета.* Petrograd, Leningrad, 1918—1935. *CSt-H*

27. *Красная новь.* Moscow, 1921—1942. *NNC CSt-H BS WB*

28. *Ленинцы.* Archangel, 1922—1925. *Location unknown*

29. *The Living Age.* Boston, n. d. *CSt-H NNU*

30. *Молодая гвардия.* Moscow, 1922—1941. *NN CSt-H*

31. *На путях к новой школе.* Moscow, n. d. *NN CSt-H WB*

32. *Nachrichtendienst (Internationale Sozialistische Kommission).* Stockholm, 1917—1918. *CSt-H*

33. *Народное просвещение.* Moscow, 1918—1931. *CSt-H BS WB*

34. *Народный учитель.* Moscow, 1917—1919; 1924—1935; 1939—1941. *Location unknown*

35. *Die Neue Zeit; Wochenschrift der deutschen Sozialdemokratie.* Stuttgart, 1883—1923. *NNC UFU*

36. *New Statesman and Nation.* London, 1931—1950. *CSt-H*

37. *Новый мир.* New York, 1911—? *NN CSt-H*

38. *Печать и революция.* Moscow, 1921—1930. *CSt-H*

39. *Под знаменем коммунизма.* Leningrad, 1921—1927. *Location unknown*

40. *Под знаменем марксизма.* Moscow, 1922—1944. *NNC CSt-H*

41. *Правда, Орган Центрального Комитета . . .* St. Petersburg, Moscow, 1917—. *Available in various libraries*

42. *Пролетарская революция; Исторический журнал испарта.* Moscow, 1921—1936. *NN NNC CSt-H BS WB*

43. *Просвещение; Ежемесячный общественно-политический и литературный журнал марксистского направления.* St. Petersburg, 1911—1917. *NNC CSt-H*

44. *Рабочий корреспондент.* Moscow, 1924—1941. *Location unknown*

45. *Революция и культура.* Moscow, 1927—1930. *NN*

46. *Революция права.* Moscow, 1927—1929. *NNC CSt-H WB*

47. *Революционный Восток.* Moscow, 1927—1937. *NN CSt-H BIW*

48. *Russische Korrespondenz.* Berlin, 1920—1922. *NNC CSt-H BS UFU WB NS-U*

49. *Социал-демократ; Центральный орган Российской социал-демократической рабочей партии.* Vilna, Paris, Geneva, 1908—1917. *NNC*

50. *Социал-демократ.* Moscow, 1917—1918. *CSt-H*

51. *Soviet Russia.* New York, Chicago, 1919—1924. *CSt-H IEUS*

52. *Спартак.* Moscow, 1917. *Location unknown*

53. *Спутник большевика.* Kursk, 1925—1928. *Location unknown*

54. *Спутник коммуниста.* Moscow, 1924—1930. *CSt-H*

55. *Ставрополье.* Stavrople, 1923—1926. *Location unknown*

56. *Stormklockan.* Stockholm, 1908—? *Location unknown*

57. *De Tribune.* Amsterdam, 1907—1937. *Location unknown*

58. *Unter dem Banner des Marxismus.* Vienna, Berlin, 1925—1934, (irregular). *CSt-H UFU*

59. *Вестник 2-го конгресса Коммунистического Интернационала* [issued as a supplement to *Правда* during the sessions of the Second Congress of the Comintern]. Moscow, 1920. *Available in various libraries*

60. *Вестник агитации и пропаганды.* Moscow, 1920—1922. *CSt-H*

61. *Вестник Коммунистической Академии.* Moscow, 1922—1935. *NN CSt-H BM-P*

62. *Вестник Социалистической Академии.* Petrograd, Moscow, 1922—1935. *CSt-H WB BS BIW BM-P*

63. *Власть Советов.* Moscow, 1917—1938. *CSt-H*

64. *За работой.* Moscow, 1922—1931. *Location unknown*

65. *Звезда.* Minsk, 1923. *Location unknown*

CHRONOLOGICAL BIBLIOGRAPHY

1906—1910

1 Теория развития народного хозяйства. N. p., n. d.

This article was written between 1906 and 1910 when Bukharin was a student at Moscow University. It was a critique of a book by P. Maslov of the same title, and the article was printed in a student journal, of which there is no extant record. The sole reference to the article is in Bukharin's biographical sketch in *Большая Советская Энциклопедия* (1st ed.), VIII, pp. 271—284.

1912

2 13-й съезд Итальянской социалистической партии. In: *Просвещение,* no. 8—9, 1912, pp. 38—48.

1912—1913

3 Политическая экономия рантье . . .

Begun in 1912—1913, but not completed and published until 1919. See no. 239.

1913

4 Борьба за всеобщее избирательное право Венгрии. In: *Просвещение,* no. 5, 1913, pp. 51—56.

5 Фокус-покусы г-на Струве (Петр Струве, «Хозяйство и цена», ч. 1: «Хозяйство и общество; цена — ценность», М., изд. В. П. Рябушинского, 1913). In: *Просвещение,* no. 12, 1913, pp. 81–89.

6 Карл Маркс и современная политическая экономия буржуазии. In: *Просвещение,* no, 7/8, 1913, pp. 29–43.

This article was incorporated in 1919 into *Политическая экономия рантье* as Chapter I. See no. 239.

7 Eine Ökonomie ohne Wert.

Written in 1913 for *Die Neue Zeit*, but not published until 1914. See no. 10.

8 Партейтаг австрийско-немецкой социал-демократии (к очередному партейтагу в Вене в 1913 г.). In: *Просвещение,* no. 11, 1913, pp. 38–41.

9 Теория либерального социализма. In: *Атака* . . . See no. 460.

This article was probably written in 1913, but it was not published until 1924 in *Атака,* where it was prefaced by the statement that this "critical article against Professor Oppenheimer, written for . . . *[Die Neue Zeit]* appears for the first time. (It was lost at the beginning of the war and was only recently found and returned to me from Germany through the kind assistance of the *Pravda* correspondent, Comrade Hamm.)" The article is a review and critique of Franz Oppenheimer's *Die soziale Frage und der Sozialismus; Eine kritische Auseinandersetzung mit der marxistischen Teorie* (Jena: Verlag von G. Fischer, 1912). The date of publication of Oppenheimer's book and the reference to the loss of the article would place its writing probably in 1913.

1914

10 Eine Ökonomie ohne Wert. In: *Die Neue Zeit*, XXXII, 1913/1914, Bd. 1, no. 22, pp. 806–816; no. 23, pp. 850–858.

This article was first published in German and then republished in 1922 and 1924 in Russian as Политическая экономия без ценности, as below.

Also in:
Политическая экономия без ценности. In: *Основные проблемы политической политики. Сборник статей, под редакцией и с предисловием С. Дволайского и И. Рубина.* Москва—Петроград, n. p., 1922; also: Москва, n. p., 1924.

Атака . . . See no. 460.

11 Теоретическое примиренчество. In: *Атака* . . . See no. 460.

This article was written for the journal *Просвещение* in 1914, but it was not published until 1924, when it was included in the collection of articles, *Атака* . . .

12 Теория субъективной ценности Бем-Баверка. In: *Просвещение,* no. 3, 1914, pp. 34—43.

This article was incorporated in 1919 into Chapters II and III of *Политическая экономия рантье* (see no. 239) and was reprinted separately in 1924 in *Атака.*

Also in:
Атака . . . See no. 460.

1915

13 Мировое хозяйство и империализм. In: *Коммунист,* no 1/2, 1915, pp. 4—44.

This article was Bukharin's original statement of his theory of imperialism, of which the later book of the same title was an elaboration (see no. 82). The basic ideas expressed by both works anticipated Lenin's views on imperialism and influenced them, though Lenin never fully acknowledged his indebtedness to Bukharin and instead receives today the credit for having originated the Bolshevik doctrine of imperialism as the highest stage of capitalism with its various implications for Communist revolutionary theory.

14 [Platform submitted by Nikolai Bukharin, Yurii Piatakov, and Evgeniia Bosh to the Central Committee of the Bolshevik Party in November 1915.] In: *Очерки по истории Октябрьской революции.* Ред. М. Н. Покровский. 2 т. Москва—Ленинград, Гос. изд., 1927. I, pp. 514—516. *NNC*

Also in:
Olga Hess Gankin and H. H. Fisher, *The Bolsheviks and the World War; the Origins of the Third International.* Stanford, Calif., Stanford University Press, 1940. 856 p., pp. 221—223.

15 [Resolution on the tasks of the party.] by Bukharin, *et al.* In: Бернская конференция 1915 года, in *Пролетарская революция,* no. 5 (40), May, 1925, pp. 134—193.

On pp. 170—172 this article provides the text of the resolution presented to the 1915 Berne Conference by the so-called "Baugy" group of Bolsheviks, of which Bukharin was a member.

Also in:
Olga Hess Gankin and H. H. Fisher, *The Bolsheviks and the World War; the Origins of the Third International.* Stanford, Calif., Stanford University Press, 1940. 856 p., pp. 189—191.

16 **Тезисы Н. И. Бухарина, предложенные им на Бернской конференции заграничных секций РСДРП.** In: *Пролетарская революция,* no. 1 (96), 1930, p. 44.

Also in:
Ленинский сборник. Москва, Институт Маркса-Энгельса-Ленина, 1924—1925, XXVII (1934), p. 198.

Olga Hess Gankin and H. H. Fisher, *The Bolsheviks and the World War; The Origins of the Third International.* Stanford, Calif., Stanford University Press, 1940. 856 p., pp. 187—189.

Both of these volumes available at various libraries.

17 **[Theses on the national question submitted by Nikolai Bukharin, Yurii Piatakov, and Evgeniia Bosh to the Central Committee of the Bolshevik Party in November 1915.]** In: *Очерки по истории Октябрьской революции.* Ред. М. Н. Покровский. 2 т. Москва—Ленинград, Гос. изд., 1927. I, pp. 516–518. *NNC*

Also in:
Olga Hess Gankin and H. H. Fisher, *The Bolsheviks and the World War; The Origins of the Third International.* Stanford, Calif., Stanford University Press, 1940. 856 p., pp 219—221.

1916

18 **Бронированный кулак поднимается . . .** In: *Новый мир,* no. 852, Dec. 7, 1916, p. 3.

19 **Что такое социализм?** In: *Новый мир,* no. 870, Dec. 28, 1916, p. 2.

20 **Дороговизна и капитализм.** In: *Новый мир,* no. 826, Nov. 7, 1916, p. 4.

21 **Где спасение маленьких наций?** In: *Новый мир,* no. 863, Dec. 20, 1916, p. 4.

22 Государственный капитализм и марксизм. In: *Новый мир,* no. 848, Dec. 2, 1916, pp. 4, 6.

23 Der imperialistische Raubstaat. In: *Jugend-Internationale,* no. 6, Dec. 1, 1916, pp. 7–9.

This article was one of the abbreviated versions of К теории империалистического государства published by Bukharin under the pseudonym, "Nota-bene," after Lenin refused to publish it in his journal, *Социал-демократ,* because it allegedly contained "semi-anarchist" errors. See also nos. 24, 25, 26, 29, 30, 583.

24 Der imperialistische Staat. In: *Arbeiterpolitik,* no. 25, Dec. 9, 1916, pp. 193—195.

This article was one of the abbreviated versions of К теории империалистического государства published by Bukharin after Lenin refused to publish it in his journal, *Социал-демократ,* because it allegedly contained "semi-anarchist" errors. See also nos. 23, 25, 26, 29, 30, 583.

25 К теории империалистического государства. In: *Революция права,* (1925). See no. 583.

This article was written in 1916, but it was not published in its entirety until 1925. In it Bukharin analyzed the origin, evolution, and destiny of the modern capitalist state and its role during and following a proletarian revolution, anticipating Lenin's position on the state expressed a year later in his *State and Revolution,* which was greatly influenced by Bukharin's pioneer study. The article was submitted to Lenin for publication in his journal, *Социал-демократ,* but it was rejected because Lenin alleged it contained "semi-anarchist" errors, an allegation he later withdrew. Bukharin published condensed versions of it during 1916 and 1917 in *Jugend-Internationale* (see no. 23), *Arbeiterpolitik* (see no. 24), *De Tribune* (see no. 29), *Новый мир* (see no. 30), *Klassekampen,* and *Stormklockan.* In 1925 the original article was published in full with an explanatory footnote which revealed additional details of the controversy and its aftermath. See no. 26 for a reference to the correspondence exchanged between Lenin and Bukharin on the dispute.

26 [Letters exchanged between Bukharin and Lenin concerning their dispute over Lenin's refusal to publish Bukharin's article, К теории империалистического государства.] In: Из материалов Института Маркса-Энгельса-Ленина, in *Большевик,* no. 22, Nov. 30, 1932.

See annotation for no. 25 on the dispute between Bukharin and Lenin.

27 Мир. In: *Новый мир,* no. 861, Dec. 18, 1916, p. 3.

28 **Наступление или отступление?** In: *Новый мир,* no. 847, Dec. 1, 1916, p. 4.

29 **De Nieuwe Lyveigenschap.** In: *De Tribune,* Nov. 25, 1916.

An abbreviated version of К теории империалистического государства, published after Lenin rejected the article on grounds that it contained "semi-anarchist" errors. See no. 583; see also nos. 23, 24, 25, 30.

30 **Новое рабство.** In: *Новый мир,* no. 830, Nov. 11, 1916, p. 4.

An abbreviated version of К теории империалистического государства, published after Lenin rejected the article on grounds that it contained "semi-anarchist" errors. See no. 583; see also nos. 23, 24, 25, 29.

31 **Право стачек в опасности.** In: *Новый мир,* no. 855, Dec. 11, 1916, p. 3.

32 **«Прогрессивные цивилизаторы» или бандиты.** In: *Новый мир,* no. 843, Nov. 27, 1916, p. 4.

33 **Протекционизм и рабочий класс.** In: *Новый мир,* no. 836, Nov. 18, 1916, p. 4.

34 **«Рождество твое, Христе, боже наш!»** In: *Новый мир,* no. 867, Dec. 25, 1916, p. 4.

35 **Всеобщая лига мира, третейские суды и разоружение.** In: *Новый мир,* no. 869, Dec. 27, 1916, p. 4.

36 **Всероссийская грабиловка.** In: *Новый мир,* no. 838, Nov. 21, 1916, p. 4.

37 **Золото и кровь.** In: *Новый мир,* no. 857, Dec. 13, 1916, p. 4.

1917

38 **19-е октября в Московских советах.** In: *Социал-демократ,* no. 189, Oct. 21 (Nov. 3), 1917.

39 **Американская социалистическая партия, мир и интернационал.** In: *Новый мир,* no. 881, Jan. 10, 1917, p. 4.

40 **Биржевая игра и «политика».** In: *Новый мир,* no. 879, Jan. 8, 1917, p. 4.

41 **Борьба против войны во время войны.** In: *Новый мир,* no. 960, Apr. 10, 1917, p. 4.

42 **Буржуазные патриоты и «заем свободы».** In: *Социал-демократ,* no. 65, May 26 (June 8), 1917.

Also in:
На подступах к Октябрю . . . See no. 691.

43 **Черносотенные «социалисты».** In: *Социал-демократ,* no. 201, Nov. 5 (18), 1917.

Also in:
На подступах к Октябрю . . . See no. 691.

44 **Что хотят большевики?** In: *Социал-демократ,* no. 197, Nov. 1 (14), 1917.

Also in:
На подступах к Октябрю . . . See no. 691.

45 **Что сулит миру новый год?** In: *Новый мир,* no. 873, Jan. 1, 1917, p. 4.

46 **Что такое финансовый капитал?** In: *Новый мир*, no. 892, Jan. 23, 1917, p. 4.

47 **Чудовищное предательство.** In: *Социал-демократ*, no. 179, Oct. 10 (23), 1917.

Also in:
На подступах к Октябрю ... See no. 691.

48 **До каких пор ждать?** In: *Социал-демократ*, no. 58, May 18 (31), 1917.

Also in:
На подступах к Октябрю ... See no. 691.

49 **Экономическая политика промышленников, Московское совещание и демократия.** In: *Спартак*, no. 6, Aug. 18 (31), 1917.

Also in:
На подступах к Октябрю ... See no. 691.

50 **Экономический развал и война.** In: *Спартак*, no. 3, June 25 (July 8), 1917.

Also in:
На подступах к Октябрю ... See no. 691.

51 **Экономика и политика.** In: *Социал-демократ*, no. 190, Oct. 22 (Nov. 4), 1917.

Also in:
На подступах к Октябрю ... See no. 691.

52 **Еще одно «освобождение».** In: *Социал-демократ*, no. 72, June 3 (16), 1917.

Also in:
На подступах к Октябрю ... See no. 691.

53 **Еще раз о товарище Ленине.** In: *Социал-демократ*, no. 100, July 6 (19), 1917.

Also in:
На подступах к Октябрю ... See no. 691.

54 **Где контр-революция?** In: *Социал-демократ*, no. 70, June 1 (14), 1917.

Also in:
На подступах к Октябрю ... See no. 691.

55 **Герой лжи и подлога.** In: *Социал-демократ*, no. 199, Nov. 3 (16), 1917.

Also in:
На подступах к Октябрю ... See no. 691.

56 **Государственный контроль над производством и русская буржуазия.** In: *Социал-демократ*, no. 64, May 25 (June 7), 1917.

Also in:
На подступах к Октябрю ... See no. 691.

57 **Грядущая война и милитаризация Америки.** In: *Новый мир*, no. 913, Feb. 16, 1917, p. 4.

58 **Громят советы.** In: *Социал-демократ*, no. 190, Oct. 22 (Nov. 4), 1917.

Also in:
На подступах к Октябрю ... See no. 691.

59 **Иезуитский штаб контр-революции.** In: *Социал-демократ*, no. 145, Aug. 29 (Sept. 11), 1917.

Also in:
На подступах к Октябрю ... See no. 691.

60 **Из-за чего борьба?** In: *Социал-демократ*, no. 195, Oct. 30 (Nov. 12), 1917.

Also in:
На подступах к Октябрю ... See no. 691.

61 **К пересмотру партийной программы.** In: *Спартак*, no. 4, Aug. 10 (23), 1917.

62 **К социализму.** In: *Социал-демократ,* no. 194, Oct. 27 (Nov. 9), 1917.

Also in:
На подступах к Октябрю ... See no. 691.

63 **К убийству Распутина.** In: *Новый мир,* no. 876, Jan. 4, 1917, p. 4.

64 **К вопросу о земельных захватах.** In: *Спартак,* no. 7, Sept. 3 (16), 1917.

Also in:
На подступах к Октябрю ... See no. 691.

65 **Кадетский съезд.** In: *Социал-демократ,* no. 185, Oct. 17 (30), 1917.

Also in:
На подступах к Октябрю ... See no. 691.

66 **Как должны бороться за мир рабочие Америки?** In: *Новый мир,* no. 883, Jan. 12, 1917, p. 4.

67 **Каледин и Авксентьев.** In: *Социал-демократ,* no. 198, Nov. 2 (15), 1917.

Also in:
На подступах к Октябрю ... See no. 691.

68 **Классовая борьба и революция в России.** Москва, Московский комитет и Областное бюро, 1917. 48 p.

NN CSt-H DLC RZIA

This pamphlet was written just after the July uprising in Petrograd in 1917.

Other editions:
Петроград, Петроградский Совет рабочих и красноармейских депутатов, 1919. 56 p. *DLC CSt-H*
Москва, Коммунист, 1919. 155 p. *DLC*
Омск, n. p., 1920. 31 p.
Иркутск, n. p., 1920. 64 p.
Красноярск, Енисейское губернское агентство ВЦИК, 19-? 57 p. *CSt-H*

Класова боротьба й революція в Росії. N. p., Державне вид-во України, 1923. 55 p. *MH*

Der Klassenkampf und die Revolution in Russland. Moskau, n. p., 1918. 83 p. *NN NNC DS OFU-W UFU*

Berlin, A. Seehof, 1920. 104 p. *NN MH IU CSt-H*

Petrograd, Die Kommunistische Internationale, 1920. 71 p. *NN NNC InU*

Osztályharc és Forradalom Oroszországban. Budapest, A Kommunisták Magyarországi Pártja, 1919. 62 p. *CSt-H*

Luokkataistelu ja Venäjänvallankumous. Stockholm, n. p., 1919. 64 p. *CSt-H*

Pietari, n. p., 1919. 64 p. *CSt-H*

Also in:

От крушения царизма до падения буржуазии. See no. 161.

Der Klassenkampf und die Revolution in Russland. In: *Russische Korrespondenz,* I, Bd. 2, no. 14—16, Oct., 1920, pp. 758—787.

Der Klassenkampf und die Revolution in Russland. In: *Vom Sturze des Zarismus bis zum Sturze der Bourgeoisie.* See no. 161.

The Grouping of the Classes before March. In: *Inprecor,* VII, no. 20, 1927.

69 Клеветники. In: *Социал-демократ,* no. 62, May 23 (June 5), 1917.

Also in:

На подступах к Октябрю . . . See no. 691.

70 Крах империалистического правительства. In: *Социал-демократ,* no. 194, Oct. 27 (Nov. 9), 1917.

Also in:

На подступах к Октябрю . . . See no. 691.

71 Кризис власти. In: *Социал-демократ,* no. 118, July 27 (Aug. 9), 1917.

Also in:

На подступах к Октябрю . . . See no. 691.

72 Крушение капитализма. In: *Спартак,* no. 10, 1917.

73 Либералы и городские служащие. In: *Социал-демократ,* no. 59, May 19 (June 1), 1917.

Also in:

На подступах к Октябрю . . . See no. 691.

74 **Манифест Российской социал-демократической рабочей партии.** In: . . . *Шестой съезд РСДРП(б).* See no. 106.

Also in:
На подступах к Октябрю . . . See no. 691.

75 **Манифест военно-революционного комитета Московских советов рабочих и солдатских депутатов ко всем гражданам Москвы.** In: *Социал-демократ*, no. 200, Nov. 4 (17), 1917.

Also in:
На подступах к Октябрю . . . See no. 691.

76 **Маски долой.** In: *Социал-демократ*, no. 198, Nov. 2 (15), 1917.

Also in:
На подступах к Октябрю . . . See no. 691.

77 **Мелкие заметки.** In: *Социал-демократ*, no. 180, Oct. 11 (24), 1917.

Also in:
На подступах к Октябрю . . . See no. 691.

78 **Международная конкуренция.** In: *Новый мир,* no. 917, Feb. 21, 1917, p. 4.

79 **Международная революция.** In: *Социал-демократ*, no. 178, Oct. 8 (21), 1917.

Also in:
На подступах к Октябрю . . . See no. 691.

80 **Международное хозяйство и борьба государств.** In: *Новый мир,* no. 1071, Aug. 17, 1917, p. 4.

81 **Министерские мероприятия.** In: *Социал-демократ*, no. 83, June 16 (29), 1917.

Also in:
На подступах к Октябрю . . . See no. 691.

82 Мировое хозяйство и империализм (экономический очерк). Москва, Гос. изд., 1917. 174 p. *CtY WaU*

This book was an elaboration of ideas first expressed in 1915 and published in that year in abbreviated form (see no. 13). Bukharin's theory of imperialism, most fully and systematically expressed in this study, anticipated Lenin's own similar views by more than a year, and Lenin's indebtedness to Bukharin for some of his own ideas on the subject are incontestable, though Lenin never fully acknowledged his debt to Bukharin and is generally credited today as the author of the official communist theory of imperialism.

Other editions:

Петербург, Прибой, 1918. 115 p. *NNC CSt-H MH ICU InU*
Петербург, n. p., 1922. 109 p.
Москва, Гос. изд., 1923. 174 p. *NN NNC MH DLC*
Петроград, Прибой, 1923. 111 p. *CU*
Москва—Петроград, n. p., 1923. 174 p.
Москва—Петроград, n. p., 1923. 174 p.
Москва—Ленинград, n. p., 1926. 136 p.
Москва, Московский рабочий, 1927. 172 p. (С предисловием В. И. Ленина). *NNC*

Imperialismus und Weltwirtschaft. Mit einem Vorwort von Lenin. Wien—Berlin, Verlag für Literatur und Politik, 1929. 193 p. *CSt-H MH CtY IU OFU-S*

L'Économie Mondiale et l'Impérialisme; Ésquisse Économique. Paris, Éditions Sociales Internationales, 1928. 178 p. *NNC IU CSt-H*
Paris, Impr. Centrale, 1928. 178 p. *UL-H*

Imperialism and World Economy; with an Introduction by V. I. Lenin. New York, International Publishers, 1929. 173 p. *NNC MH NjP CLU ICU InU IU OCl WaU CSt-H*
London, M. Lawrence, 1930. 173 p. *CtY CU*

La Economia Mundial y el Imperialismo. Trad. de Luis F. Bustamente. Madrid, n. p., 1930. 276 p.

Világgazdaság és Imperialismus; Közgazdasági Tanulmány. Budapest, A Szocialista-Kommunista Munkások Magyarországi Pártja, 1919. 148 p. *CSt-H*

Анархия мирового хозяйства. In: *Марксистская хрестоматия* ... See no. 496.
Мощь трестов. In: *Марксистская хрестоматия* ... See no. 496.
От мирового капитализма к мировому социализму. In: *Марксистская хрестоматия* ... See no. 496.

Also in:
Атака ... See no. 460.

83 На краю пропасти. In: *Новый мир,* no. 902, Feb. 3, 1917, p. 4.

84 Натиск капиталистов. In: *Социал-демократ*, no. 92, June 27 (July 10), 1917.

Also in:
На подступах к Октябрю ... See no. 691.

85 **Неизбежный крах.** In: *Новый мир,* no. 945, Mar. 24, 1917, p. 4.

86 **Нота временного правительства.** In: *Социал-демократ*, no. 73, June 4 (17), 1917.

Also in:
На подступах к Октябрю ... See no. 691.

87 **Новая революция и международный капитал.** In: *Социал-демократ*, no. 196, Oct. 31 (Nov. 13), 1917.

Also in:
На подступах к Октябрю ... See no. 691.

88 **О Московских событиях. Речь тов. Н. И. Бухарина на заседании всеросс. цент. исполн. комитета советов рабоч. и солдатск. депутатов; II созыва.** In: *На подступах к Октябрю* ... See no. 691.

This speech was delivered on Nov. 6 (19), 1917.

89 **О наступлении (из стенограммы заседания исп. ком. с. р. и с. д. 21 июня).** In: *Социал-демократ*, no. 90, June 24 (July 7), 1917.

Also in:
На подступах к Октябрю ... See no. 691.

90 **О наступлении на фронте.** In: *Социал-демократ*, no. 88, June 23 (July 6), 1917.

Also in:
На подступах к Октябрю ... See no. 691.

91 **О падении ценности русского рубля.** In: *Новый мир,* no. 888, Jan. 18, 1917, p. 3.

92 **«Общенациональные задачи» и гражданская война.** In: *Спартак*, no. 7, Sept. 3 (16), 1917.

Also in:
На подступах к Октябрю ... See no. 691.

93 **Они недовольны.** In: *Социал-демократ*, no. 48, May 5 (18), 1917.

Also in:
На подступах к Октябрю ... See no. 691.

94 **Организованное творчество.** In: *Социал-демократ*, no. 66, May 27 (June 9), 1917.

Also in:
На подступах к Октябрю ... See no. 691.

95 **Організуйтесь!** Cleveland, Ohio, Вид. Української Федерації Американської соціяліст. партії. The Robitnyk, 1917. 18 p.

Also in:
На подступах к Октябрю ... See no. 691.

96 **Парижская коммуна и революционная Россия (историческая параллель).** In: *Социал-демократ*, no. 94, June 29 (July 12), 1917.

Also in:
На подступах к Октябрю ... See no. 691.

97 **Пацифизм и социалдемократия.** In: *Новый мир,* no. 911, Feb. 14, 1917, p. 4.

98 **Перспективы революции.** In: *Новый мир,* no. 948, Mar. 27, 1917, p. 4.

99 **Петроградский Совет р. и с. д. и армия.** In: *Социал-демократ*, no. 46, May 3 (16), 1917.

Also in:
На подступах к Октябрю ... See no. 691.

100 **Планы генералов.** In: *Социал-демократ*, no. 145, Aug. 29 (Sept. 11), 1917.

Also in:
На подступах к Октябрю ... See no. 691.

101 **По поводу наступления.** In: *Социал-демократ*, no. 87, June 21 (July 4), 1917.

Also in:
На подступах к Октябрю... See no. 691.

102 **По поводу съезда советов рабочих и солдатских депутатов.** In: *Социал-демократ*, no. 77, June 9 (22), 1917.

Also in:
На подступах к Октябрю... See no. 691.

103 **Поражение или победа?** In: *Социал-демократ*, no. 103, July 9 (22), 1917.

Also in:
На подступах к Октябрю... See no. 691.

104 **Путаница или обман.** In: *Новый мир*, no. 951, Mar. 30, 1917, p. 4.

105 **Развернутый фронт.** In: *Социал-демократ*, no. 186, Oct. 18 (31), 1917.

Also in:
На подступах к Октябрю... See no. 691.

106 **[Remarks of Bukharin.]** In: *Протоколы съездов и конференций Всесоюзной Коммунистической партии (б); Шестой съезд РСДРП(б).* Москва, Партийное издательство, 1934. 371 p.

Available in various libraries.

107 **[Remarks of Bukharin.]** In: *Протоколы Центрального Комитета РСДРП. Август 1917 — февраль 1918.* Москва—Ленинград, Гос. изд., 1929. 309 p.

Available in various libraries.

108 **Российская революция и ее судьбы.** In: *Спартак*, no. 1, May 20 (June 2), 1917.

Also in:
На подступах к Октябрю... See no. 691.

109 **The Russian Revolution and Its Significance.** In: *The Class Struggle*, I, May-June, 1917, pp. 14–22.

110 **Русское наступление и цели союзников.** In: *Социал-демократ*, no. 67, May 28 (June 10), 1917.

Also in:
На подступах к Октябрю ... See no. 691.

111 **Слова и дела.** In: *Социал-демократ*, no. 74, June 6 (19), 1917.

Also in:
На подступах к Октябрю ... See no. 691.

112 **Соединенные Штаты и великодержавная политика.** In: *Новый мир*, no. 904, Feb. 6, 1917, p. 4.

113 **Союзы государств и тайная дипломатия.** In: *Новый мир*, no. 925, Mar. 2, 1917, p. 4.

114 **«Сотрудничество всех классов».** In: *Социал-демократ*, no. 108, July 15 (28), 1917.

Also in:
На подступах к Октябрю ... See no. 691.

115 **Советы прежде и теперь.** In: *Спартак*, no. 9, Oct. 12 (25), 1917.

Also in:
На подступах к Октябрю ... See no. 691.

116 **Торжественное заявление.** In: *Социал-демократ*, no. 84, June 17 (30), 1917.

Also in:
На подступах к Октябрю ... See no. 691.

117 **Тресты, империализм и дороговизна.** In: *Новый мир,* no. 923, Feb. 28, 1917, p. 4.

Also in:
На подступах к Октябрю... See no. 691.

118 **Три направления в старой социал-демократии.** In: *Социал-демократ,* no. 56, May 16 (29), 1917.

Also in:
На подступах к Октябрю... See no. 691.

119 **Троица «миролюбия» лицемирия.** In: *Новый мир,* no. 905, Feb. 7, 1917, p. 4.

120 **Урядники или педагоги?** In: *Новый мир,* no. 918, Feb. 22, 1917, p. 3.

121 **Военная дороговизна.** In: *Социал-демократ,* no. 53, May 11 (24), 1917.

Also in:
На подступах к Октябрю... See no. 691.

122 **Война и революционные социал-демократы.** In: *Спартак,* no. 1, May 20 (June 2), 1917.

123 **Восстановление самодержавия?** In: *Социал-демократ,* no. 179, Oct. 10 (23), 1917.

Also in:
На подступах к Октябрю... See no. 691.

124 **Вперед.** In: *Спартак,* no. 2, June 6 (19), 1917.

Also in:
На подступах к Октябрю... See no. 691.

1918

125 **Анархизм и научный коммунизм.** In: *Коммунист*, no. 2, April 27, 1918, pp. 11–14.

Other editions:

Anarchismus und wissenschaftlicher Kommunismus. Aus dem Russischen übersetzt von W. R.; Vorwort von Fritz Sturm. Hamburg, Willaschek, 1919. 15 p. *NN MH UFU*

Hamburg, Willaschek, 1920. 15 p.

Anarchia e Communismo Scientifico. Roma, n. p., 1922. 15 p.

Anarquismo y Comunismo Cientifico; Traducción de A. Stirner y R. Carrillo. Barcelona, La Batalla, 1923. 16 p. *NN*

Mexico, D. F., Biblioteca del Partido Communista de Mexico, 1925. 30 p. *NN*

Also in:

Христян Г. Раковскі, *Інтернаціонал і війна. З додатком: Анархизм и науковий комунізм, Н. Бухаріна. Пер. М. Андрейчук.* New York, Видання Української Федерації Американської Соціялістичної партії. З друкарні «Робітника», 1919, 41 р. *NN*

126 **Армия в советской республике.** Пермь, n. p., 1918. 12 p.

127 **Блестящие действия чехо-словацких и казачьих войск.** In: *Правда*, no. 154, July 25, 1918, p. 1.

128 **Часовой пролетарской революции.** In: *Правда*, no. 185, Aug. 31, 1918, p. 1.

129 **Через горнило империалистической войны (к 4-х летию мировой войны),** by N. Bukharin, B. Volin, A. Lomov, and N. Ossinskii. Москва—Петроград, Коммунист, 1918. 40 p. *RZIA*

Bukharin's contribution to this collection includes: Гинденбург, Фош, Алексеев (1918?). Крепостники XX века (1918?). На мировых путях (1918?).

130 **«Демократический» жандарм.** In: *Правда*, no. 253, Nov. 22, 1918, p. 1.

131 **Долой международних разбойников!** Москва, «Волна», 1918. 32 p.
NN DLC CSt-H BDIC RZIA

Other editions:

Москва, Коммунист, 1918. 32 p. *CSt-H*
Петроград, n. p., 1918. 8 p.
Екатериноград, n. p., 1918. 32 p.

Долу международните разбойници. Москва, Комуна, 1918. 32 p.
Alas Kansainväliset Rosvot! Pitarie, n. p., 1919. 32 p. *CSt-H*
Le a Nemzetköz! Rablókkal! Forditotta: Hancsok Kalman. Budapest, A Magyarorszagi Szocialista Partja, 1919. 31 p. *CSt-H*

132 **Экономическая борьба на Тихом океане.** In: *Правда*, no. 278, Dec. 21, 1918, p. 1.

133 **Экономическая диктатура пролетариата.** In: *Правда*, no. 276, Dec. 19, 1918, p. 1.

134 **Экономическое удушение революции.** In: *Правда*, no. 280, Dec. 24, 1924, p. 1.

135 **Это нужно сделать немедленно.** In: *Правда*, no. 252, Nov. 21, 1918, p. 1.

136 **Гинденбург, Фош, Алексеев.** In: *Через горнило . . .* See no. 129.

137 **Города должны принадлежать рабочим.** In: *Правда*, no. 182, Aug. 27, 1918, p. 1.

138 **Июльская годовщина.** In: *Правда*, no. 149, July 19, 1918, p. 1.

139 **Июльские дни 1917 г.,** by N. Bukharin and G. Zinoviev. Москва, Изд. Всероссийского исполнительного комитета Советов р. с. кр. и казач. депутатов, 1918. 15 p.
NNC RZIA

140 **Итоги и перспективы.** In: *Правда*, no. 227, Jan. 13, 1918, p. 1.

141 **Из программы коммунистов.** See no. 167.

142 **К итогам съезда рабочей кооперации.** In: *Правда*, no. 275, Dec. 18, 1918, p. 1.

143 **Казни солдат революции.** In: *Правда*, no. 175, Aug. 18, 1918, p. 1.

144 **Der Klassenkampf und die Revolution in Russland.** (1917.) See no. 68,

145 **Коалиция или военная диктатура.** In: *Правда*, no. 210, Oct. 1, 1918, p. 1.

146 **Конец империалистической войны и мировая революция.** In: *Правда*, no. 255, Nov. 24, 1918, p. 1.

147 **Крепостники XX века.** In: *Через горнило . . .* See no. 129.

148 **Ленин — Каплан, Урицкий — Канегиссер.** In: *Правда*, no. 186, Sept. 1, 1918, p. 1.

149 **Меньшевистско-генеральский блок.** In: *Правда*, no. 159, July 31, 1918, pp. 1–2.

150 **Миротворческое слово блудие.** In: *Правда*, no. 155, July 26, 1918, p. 1.

151 **Мировое хозяйство и империализм . . . (1917.)** See no. 82.

152 **Мировой раздел.** In: *Правда*, no. 194, Sept. 11, 1918, p. 1.

153 **Монарх Финляндии и торговля рабочими.** In: *Правда*, no. 151, July 21, 1918, p. 1.

154 **Московский Совет рабоч. и красноарм. деп.** In: *Правда*, no. 147, July 17, 1918, p. 3.

155 **На мировых путях.** In: *Правда*, no. 160, Aug. 1, 1918, p. 1.

Also in:
Через горнило... See no. 129.

156 **«Нейтральные» и «активные».** In: *Правда*, no. 183, Aug. 28, 1918, p. 1.

157 **Некоторые основные понятия современной экономики.** In: *Коммунист*, no. 3, May 16, 1918.

158 **Неотложная задача.** In: *Правда*, no. 179, Aug. 23, 1918, p. 1.

159 **Новое земледельческое хозяйство; что делать с землей?** Самара, n.p., 1918. 1 p.

Other editions:
Москва, n. p., 1919.

160 **От диктатуры империализма к диктатуре пролетариата (классовая борьба и революция в России).** Петроград, Прибой, 1918. 48 p.

Other editions:

Петроград, Государственная тип., 1918. 48 p. *CSt-H*

De la Dictature de l'Impérialisme à la Dictature du Prolétariat (La Lutte des Classes et la Révolution en Russie). Genève, Edition Universa, 1918. 72 p.
NN DS UL-H CSt-H

Od Diktatury Imperialismu k Diktature Proletariátu. Praha, Vytiskla Knihtiskárna-grafia, 1918(?). 68 p. *CSt-H*

Az Imperializmus Diktaturájatól a Proletárdiktaturáig. Forditotta Rajczy Reszö. Budapest, A Kommunisták Magyarországi Pártsának Kiadása, 1919. 48 p. *CSt-H*

Budapest, A Magyarországi Szocialista Partja, 1919. 53 p. *CSt-H*

Imperialismin Diktatuurista Työväen Diktatuuriin. Pietari, n. p., 1919. 63 p. *CSt-H*

Also in:

От крушения царизма... See no. 161.

Von der Diktatur des Imperialismus zur Diktatur des Proletariats. In: *Vom Sturze des Zarismus...* See no. 161.

The July Victory of the Counter-revolution. In: *Inprecor,* VII, no. 44, 1927.

The Kornilov Putsch and the Resistance of the Working Class. In: *Inprecor,* VII, no. 53, 1927.

The True Causes of the Resignation of the Cadets. In: *Inprecor,* VII, no. 41, 1927.

Славные революции и великие бунты. In: *Марксисткая хрестоматия...* See no. 496.

161 **От крушения царизма до падения буржуазии.** Москва, Коммунист, 1918.

Contents: Классовая борьба и революция в России (1917). От диктатуры империализма к диктатуре пролетариата. See nos. 68 and 160, respectively.

Other editions:

Харьков, *«Пролетарий»,* 1921. 144 p.

Харьков, *«Пролетарий»,* 1923. 144 p. *NN CSt-H CtY RZIA*

Von Sturze des Zarismus bis zum Sturze der Bourgeoisie. Zürich, "Union" Buchdruckerei, 1918. 83 p. *MH CSt-H*

Berlin, Verlag "Rote Fahne", 1919. 104 p. *NN ICU BS OFU-W*

Leipzig, Frankes Verlag, 1919. 104 p. *NNC*

162 **Отклики.** In: *Правда,* no. 261, Dec. 1, 1918, p. 1.

163 **Отклики.** In: *Правда,* no. 262, Dec. 3, 1918, p. 1.

164 **Отклики.** In: *Правда,* no. 263, Dec. 4, 1918, p. 1.

165 **Политическое обозрение; герой социал-предательства.** In: *Коммунист,* no. 1, Apr. 20, 1918, pp. 17—18.

166 **Порядок (статья для обывателей).** In: *Правда*, no. 170, Aug. 13, 1918, p. 2.

167 **Программа коммунистов (большевиков).** Москва, Коммунист, 1918. 64 p. *ICU*

Other editions:
Москва, «Волна», 1918. 64 p. *NN NNC MH DLC CSt-H CU ICU*
Вятка, n. p., 1918. 62 p.
Петроград, Петроградский Совет рабочих и красноармейских депутатов, 1919. 59 p. *NN NNC MH CSt-H*
Харьков, Центропечать, 1919. 64 p. *MH*
Нью Йорк, Издание Русской Социалистической Федерации, 1919, 24 p. *MH NjP*
Нью Йорк, Издание Русской Социалистической федерации, 1919. 19 p. *NNC*
Киев, n. p., 1919. 63 p.
Баку, Изд. Центрального Комитета А. К., 1919. 96 p.
Минск, I-я Советская типография. 1919. 63 p.
Самара, Тип. Совнархоза № 8, 1919. 64 p.
Гамбург, n. p., 1920. 64 p. *CSt-H*
Нью Йорк, Издание Центрисполкома РФКПА, 1921. 78 p. *NN WaU*

Програма Комуністів (большевиків). Москва, Российская Коммунистическая партия, 1918. 69 p. *BDIC*
New York, Видання Української федерації Американської социялістичної партії, 1919. 128 p. *NN DLC CSt-H MH*

Programm der Kommunisten (Bolschewiki). Bern-Belp, Promachos-Verlag, 1918. 117 p. *NN CtY IU CSt-H*
Essen, n. p., 1918. 90 p.
Bern, Fritz Platten, 1918. 117 p. *CtY*
Zürich, Union, 1918. 67 p. *CSt-H*
Zürich, n. p., 1918. 86 p. (Mit einem Vorwort von K. Radek) *MH InU*
Cleveland, Ohio, Toiler Publishing Association, 1918. 95 p. *NN NNC CtY*
Berlin, Verlag Rote Fahne, 1919. 127 p. *MH CSt-H*
Berlin, Verlag Gesellschaft und Erziehung, 1919. 194 p. *InU CLU NjP CSt-H*
Berlin, A. Hoffman, 1919. 83 p. *CSt-H*
Berlin, n. p., 1919. 128 p.
Berlin, A. Hoffman, 1919. 87 p. (With an introduction by R. *[sic]* Radek, "Die Entwicklung des Sozialismus von der Wissenschaft zur Tat", von R. *[sic]* Radek, pp. i-xxvii). *InU*
Wien, n. p., 1919. 88 p.

Other German editions are available also at: *BS UFU OFU-G OFU-W*

Program Komunistów (Bolszewików). Warszawa, n. p., 1919. 67 p. *CSt-H*
Moskva, n. p., 1920. 52 p.

Le programme des Communistes (Bolcheviki). La Chaux-du-Fonds, Impr. Coopérative, 1918. 85 p. *NN UL-H*
La Chaux-du-Fonds, Impr. Coopérative, 1919. 85 p. *CSt-H*
N. p., n. p., 1919. 88 p.

Program of the Communists (Bolshevists). N. p., United Communist Party of America, 1918. 82 p. *NN NNC CSt-H*
N. p., Communist Labor Party, 1918. 82 p. *MH NjP CU CLU IU*

Programme of the Communists (Bolsheviks). Moscow, The Group of English-Speaking Communists in Russia, 1919. 79 p. *NN MH WaU*

Programme of the World Revolution. New York, Contemporary Publishing Association, 1920. 96 p. *NN NNC MH NjP CU CtY CSt-H IU WaU*
Glasgow, Socialist Labour Press, 1920. 94 p. *CLU IU WaU DS OFU-W*
Kommunistide (Enamlaste) Programm. Petrograd, n. p. 1918. 69 p.

Il Programma dei Communisti (Bolscevichi). Milano, Soc. Editrice Avanti, 1920. 96 p.
Kommunistide (Enamlaste) Programm. Petrograd, n. p., 1918. 69 p. *NN*
Världsrevolutionens Program. Bomyndigad Översättning frän Ryskan [av Alice Wallenius]. Stockholm, Fram, 1919. 108 p. *NN CSt-H BS*
Kommunistien (Bolshevikkien) Ohjelma. Pietari, n. p., 1918. 114 p.
Stockholm, n. p., 1919. 112 p.
Komunistu-lielinieku Programa. Tulkojis K. Mika. Petrograd, n. p., 1918. 67 p.
A Kommunisták (Bolsevikiek) Programmja. Forditotta: Rudnyánszky Endre. Budapest, A Kommunisták Magyarországi Pártja, 1918. 106 p. *CSt-H*
Budapest, A. Kommunisták Magyarországi Pártja, 1919. 93 p. *CSt-H*

Also in:
Из программы коммунистов. In: *Первый народный календарь на 1919 г.* Петроград, n. p., 1919. *NNC BDIC*
Das Programm der Bolschewiki (Auszug). In: *Grundlagen und Kritik des Sozialismus.* Berlin, n. p., 1919, II, pp. 219—230.

See also *Церковь и школа в Советской Республике,* no. 185.

168 [Remarks of Bukharin at the All-Russian Constituent Assembly, January 5—6 (18—19), 1918.] In: *Архив Октябрьской Революции, 1917 г. в документах и материалах. Всероссийское учредительное собрание.* Москва—Ленинград, Гос. изд., 1930. 219 p.

The verbatim report of the single session of the Constituent Assembly, including Bukharin's remarks, is to be found on pp. 1—111.

Also in:
Вокруг Учредительного собрания. Сборник статей и документов. Петроград, Гос. изд., 1918. 50 p. *NN*
Речь на первом заседании Учредительного собрания. In: *На подступах к Октябрю ...* See no. 691.

169 [Remarks of Bukharin.] In: Пленарное заседание Московского совета рабочих, кр. и красноарм. депутатов. 8-го октября 1918 г., in *Правда,* no. 219, Oct. 11, 1918, p. 3.

170 [Remarks of Bukharin.] In: *Протоколы заседаний Центрального Исполнительного Комитета 4-го созыва.* Москва, Гос. изд., 1920. 442 p.

171 [Remarks of Bukharin.] In: *Седьмой съезд Российской Коммунистической партии. Стенографический отчет. 6—8 марта 1918 года.* Москва —Петроград, Гос. изд., 1923. 212 p.

Available in various libraries.

172 **[Remarks of Bukharin.]** In: *Труды I Всероссийского съезда Советов народного хозяйства. Стенографический отчет.* Москва, n. p., 1918. 488 p.

NN

173 **Репетиция.** In: *Правда*, no. 176, Aug. 20, 1918, p. 1.

174 **[Review of Lenin's Государство и революция.]** In: *Коммунист*, no. no. 1, Apr. 20, 1918, p. 19.

175 **[Review of Vladimir Trutkovskii's Переходный период.]** In: *Коммунист*, no. 1, Apr. 20, 1918, p. 20.

176 **Революционная Германия.** In: *Правда*, no. 251, Nov. 20, 1918, p. 1.

177 **Сельско-хозяйственные коммуны или хлебные фабрики?** In: *Правда*, no. 277, Dec. 20, 1918, p. 1.

178 **Съезд земотделов, коммун и комбедов.** In: *Правда*, no. 279, Dec. 22, 1918, p. 1.

179 **Синдикализм и коммунизм.** In: *Правда*, no. 15, Jan. 25, 1918, p. 1.

180 **Смысл событий.** In: *Правда*, no. 140, July 9, 1918, p. 1.

181 **Союз народов.** In: *Правда*, no. 222, Oct. 15, 1918, p. 1.

182 **Тезисы о текущем моменте,** by Bukharin *et al.* In: *Коммунист,* no. 1, Apr. 20, 1918, pp. 4—9.

This set of "theses" was proposed by Bukharin and other leading "Left Communists" as their counter-proposals to the policies of Lenin and the Party majority following the conclusion of the peace of Brest-Litovsk and contained their program for the future development of internal and international events.

183 **Thesen über die sozialistische Revolution und die Aufgaben das Proletariats während seiner Diktatur in Russland.** In: Internationale Sozialistische Kommission, *Nachrichtendienst,* no. 41, June 12, 1918.

This set of "theses" was requested by the German Communist Party, which smuggled in large quantities of this issue of the Zimmerwald newsletter and distributed them illegally among German workers in hopes of arousing them to a communist revolution in 1918.

184 **Царя.** In: *Правда*, no. 150, July 20, 1918, p. 1.

185 **Церковь и школа в советской республике (из программы коммунистов-большевиков).** Москва, Изд. Всероссийского Центрального Исполнительного комитета Советов р. с. к. и к. Депутатов, 1918. 16 p.

NN MH CSt-H DLC BDIC BrM

This pamphlet is a reprint of Ch. XVII of *Программа коммунистов . . .* See no. 167.

Other editions:
Нью Йорк, Русская Социалистическая Федерация, 1919. 16 p.
NN NNC MH CSt-H

Петроград, n. p., 1920. 8 p.
Омск, n. p., 1920. 7 p.
Москва, n. p., 1920.

186 **Восточная революция.** In: *Правда*, no. 192, Sept. 8, 1918, p. 1.

187 **Всеобщая дележка или коммунистическое производство?** Москва, Всероссийский Центральный Исполнительный Комитет, 1918. 8 p.
NNC BrM BDIC UL-H DS

Other editions:
Одесса, n. p., 1919. 7 p. BDIC RZIA UL-H

Општа деоба или комунистичка производива? Москва, Коммунист, 1918. 8 p. *BDIC*

188 **Zasady rewolucji socjalistycznej w Rosji.** Warszawa, n. p., 1918. 12 p.

1919

189 **«13,600».** In: *Правда*, no. 234, Oct. 10, 1919, p. 1.

190 **Alas Kansainväliset Rosvot!** (1918). See no. 131.

191 **Anarchismus und wissenschaftlicher Kommunismus.** (1918). See no. 125.

192 **[Анархізм і науковий комунізм . . .]** (1918). See no. 125.

193 **Az imperialismus diktaturájától a proletárdiktaturáig . . .** (1918). See no. 160.

194 **Азбука коммунизма; популярное объяснение программы Российской Коммунистической Партии (большевиков),** by Bukharin and Preobrazhenskii. Москва, n. p., 1919. 340 p.

See the introduction for an indication of which parts of this book were written by each co-author, respectively.

Other editions:
N. p., n. p., 1919. 283 p. *NNC*
Москва, Гос. Изд., 1920. 340 p. *MH CSt-H*
Петербург, Гос. изд., 1920. 321 p. *CSt-H InU*
Москва, Издание политического отдела 10 армии, 1920. 208 p. *CSt-H ICU MiU*
Саратов, Гос. изд., Саратовское отделение, 1920. 247 p. *NN CSt-H*
Петроград, n. p., 1920. 120 p.
Москва, n. p., 1920. 140 p.
Гамбург, n .p., 1920. 283 p.
Петербург, n. p., 1921. 322 p.
Иркутск, n. p., 1921. 164 p.
Гомель, Гос. изд., 1921. 321 p. *DLC CSt-H NjP*
Нью Йорк, Изд. Объединенной Коммунистической Партии Америки, 1921. 269 p. *NN NNC MH CtY CU CLU*
N. p., n. p., 1921. *OCl*
Одесса, n. p., 1922. 320 p.
Одесса, n. p., 1923. 264 p.
Харьков, Гос. изд. Украины, 1924. 263 p. *NN*
Харьков, Гос. изд. Украины, 1925. 319 p. *InU*

Азбука комунізма. Доступне пояснення програми Російської Комуністичної партії (большевиків). Нью Йорк, Накл. Української Федерації Комуністичної партії Америки, 1920. 319 p. *NN MH IU*

Київ, Українська Соціалістична Радянська Республіка, Всеукраїнське Державне Видавництво, 1920. 411 p. *CSt-H*

Das ABC des Kommunismus. Populäre Erläuterung des Programms der Kommunistischen Partei Russlands (Bolschewiki). Wien, Im Verlag der Kommunistischen Partei Deutschösterreichs, 1920. 2 vols. *NN MH CSt-H*
Hamburg, n. p., 1921. 346 p.
Hamburg, C. Hoym Nachfolger L. Cahnbley, 1921. 376 p. *NN NNC CSt-H*
Hamburg, C. Hoym Nachfolger, 1923. 368 p.
Petrograd, Kommunistische Internationale, 1923. 368 p. *NjP InU CSt-H DIC*

German edition also available at: *OFU-G OFU-W*

ABC du Communisme. Paris, Librairie de l'Humanité, 1925. 175 p. *CSt-H MH NjP UL-H DS*

ABC du Communisme. Éd. Nouv. Intégrale, Presentée par Sierre Broué. Paris, F. Maspero, 1963. 350 p. *CSt-H*

The ABC of Communism. By N. Bucharin and E. Preobraschensky. Translated from the German by P. Lavin. A Popular Exposition of the Programme of the Communist Party of Russia (the Bolsheviki). Glasgow, Socialist Labor Press, 1921. 165 p. *OCl CU WaU*

The ABC of Communism by N. Bucharin and E. Preobraschensky. Translated by P. Lavin. Vol. I. Detroit, The Marxian Educational Society, 1921. 136 p. [No more published] *NNC CtY NjP IU ICU*
New York, Lyceum-Literature Department, Workers Party of America, 1921, 136 p. *NN MH CtY*

The ABC of Communism. A Popular Explanation of the Program of the Communist Party of Russia by N. Bucharin and E. Preobraschensky. Translated from the Russian by Eden and Cedar Paul. London, The Communist Party of Great Britain, 1922. 422 p. *MH InU CtY CSt-H WaU*
London, The Communist Party of Great Britain, 1922. 428 p. *NN CLU*
London, The Communist Party of Great Britain, 1924. 428 p. *MH CSt-H DLC*
London, The Communist Party of Great Britain, 1927. 428 p. *NNC*

l'A.B.C. del Communismo. Parte I: Sviluppo e Decadenca del Capitalismo. Roma, n. p., 1921. 168 p.

ABC del Comunismo. Mexico, Frente Cultural, 19? 112 p. *NNC CSt-H*

El A.B.C. del Comunismo. 2nd ed. La Paz, Bolivia, Editorial Trabajo, 1954. 151 p. *MH*

El programa militar de los Comunistas. N. p., Barcelona, 1937. *CtY*

Komunisma Abezee. Kreewijas Komunistiskàs (Leelineeku) Partijas Programas Populars Istirsajums. Riga, Latwijas Komunistiskàs Grahmatu Apgahdneeziba "Spartaks", 1920. 261 p. *NN*

Kommunismin Aapinen. Kansantajuinen Esitys Venäjän Kommunistisen (Bolshevikkien). Puolueen Ohjelmasta. Stockholm, n. p., 1921. 447 p.
Kuopio, n. p., 1921. 391 p.

Kommunismus Ábécése az Oroszországe Kommunista (Bolseviki). Pàrt Programmjanak Népszerü Magyaràzata. Forditotta: Rudniánszky Endre. Moskva, n. p., 1920. 293 p.

A Kommunismus Ábécéje, irta: Bucharin és Preobrazsenszky. Wien, Verlag der Arbeiterbuchhandlung, 1922. 95 p. *CSt-H*

Komunisam Aspukki. Rassej Komunissen (Polševiksen) Parttiiên Prokrammine Têlên (Popularli Anlantarni). Chusan [Казань], n. p., 1922. 160 p.

Kyosan Shugi no ABC. Tokyo, n. p., 1952. *CtY*

Развитие капитализма и его гибель. Теоретическая часть «Азбуки коммунизма». Новониколаевск, n. p., 1923. 55 p.

От капитализма к коммунизму. Из «Азбуки коммунизма». Москва—Ленинград, n. p., 1925. 80 p.

195 **Барон и рабочий.** In: *Правда,* no. 216, Sept. 28, 1919, p. 1.

196 **Борьба международного пролетариата и господа меньшевики.** In: *Правда,* no. 54, Mar. 11, 1919, p. 1.

197 **Борьба с белыми и театр.** In: *Правда,* no. 231, Oct. 16, 1919, p. 1.

198 **Борьба с бюрократизмом.** In: *Правда,* no. 261, Nov. 21, 1919, p. 1.

199 **Диктатура пролетариата в России и мировая революция.** In: *Коммунистический Интернационал,* I, May, 1919, pp· 487–492; 613–618.

Other editions:
Диктатура пролетариата в России и мировая революция. Самара, n. p., 1925. 23 p.

Also in:
Die Diktatur des Proletariats in Russland und die Weltrevolution. In: *Die Kommunistische Internationale,* no. 4/5, Aug.—Sept., 1919, pp. 26—40.

200 **Еще раз о мире.** In: *Правда,* no. 256, Nov. 15, 1919, p. 1.

201 **Еврей и пролетариат.** In: *Правда,* no. 258, Nov. 18, 1919, p. 1.

202 **Франц Меринг.** In: *Правда,* no. 30, Feb. 9, 1919, p. 1.

203 **Где настоящая свобода?** Москва, n. p., 1919 (?), 16 p.

Other editions:
Москва, Гос. изд., 1920. 16 р. *CSt-H*
Харьков, Всеукраинское изд., 1920. 8 р. *NNC DLC CSt-H BDIC RZIA*
N. р., ЦККПЛиБ, 1920. 12 р. *CSt-H*

Де справжня свобода? N. p., n. p., 1920. 7 p. *BDIC*

204 **Гениальное пророчество.** In: *Правда,* no. 174, Aug. 8, 1919, p. 1.

205 **Гражданская война в Европе.** In: *Правда,* no. 9, Jan. 15, 1919, p. 1.

206 **Им мало крови!** In: *Правда,* no. 237, Dec. 21, 1919, p. 1.

207 **Imperialismin Diktatuurista. Työväen Diktatuurin.** (1918). See no. 160.

208 **Империалистическая похоть.** In: *Правда,* no. 187, Aug. 24, 1919, p. 1.

209 **Из программы коммунистов...** (1918). See no. 167.

210 **К вопросу о развитии производительных сил** In: *Правда,* no. 284, Dec. 18, 1919, p. 1.

211 **Der Klassenkampf und die Revolution in Russland.** (1917). See no. 68.

212 **Классовая борьба и революция в России.** (1917). See no. 68.

213 **Ко второму всероссийскому съезду профессиональных союзов.** In: *Правда,* no. 10, Jan. 16, 1919, p. 1.

214 **«Коалиция», предательство и меньшевики.** In: *Правда,* no. 172, Aug. 6, 1919, p. 1.

214a **A Kommunisták (Bolsevikiek) Programmja...** (1918). See no. 167.

215 **Kommunistien (Bolshevikien) Ohjelma.** (1918). See no. 167.

216 **Кто говорит: «Долой гражданскую войну»?** In: *Правда,* no. 212, Sept. 24, 1919, p. 1.

217 **Le a Nemzetköz! Rablókkal!** (1918). See no. 131.

218 **Лига убийц.** In: *Правда,* no. 184, Aug. 21, 1919, p. 1.

219 **Luokkataistelu ja Venäjänvallankumous.** (1917). See no. 68.

220 **Maailamn-kapitalismin Rakenne.** Stockholm, n. p., 1919. 15 p.

221 **Маленький фельетон.** In: *Правда,* no. 260, Nov. 20, 1919, p. 1.

222 **Мститель.** In: *Правда,* no. 262, Dec. 16, 1919, p. 1.

223 **Насущнейшая задача (о новых членах партии).** In: *Правда,* no. 266, Nov. 27, 1919, p. 1.

224 **Необходимый шаг вперед.** In: *Правда,* no. 4, Jan. 5, 1919, p. 1.

225 **Неукротимый вождь. Памяти товарища Либкнехта.** In: *Правда,* no. 13, Jan. 19, 1919, pp. 1–2.

Also in:
Памяти Карла Либкнехта и Розы Люксембург ... See no. 235.

226 **Новая угроза.** In: *Правда,* no. 289, Dec. 24, 1919, p. 1.

227 **Новое земледельческое хозяйство...** (1918). See no. 159.

228 **Новый декрет о чрезвычайном налоге.** In: *Правда,* no. 73, Apr. 12, 1919, p. 1.

229 **Об использовании новых членов партии.** In: *Известия*, no. 11, Dec. 31, 1919, p. 1.

230 **Обоснование партийной программы. Доклад на VIII съезде РКП.**

Delivered in 1919, this report was published separately in 1922, 1924, and 1925. See no. 393; for a complete record of Bukharin's remarks to the Eighth Congress of the Russian Communist Party, see no. 255.

231 **Osztályharc és Forradalom Oroszországban.** (1917). See no. 68.

232 **От нелегального кружка к государственной власти.** In: *На заре рабочего движения в Москве.* Москва, n. p., 1919.

233 **От ворот поворот... (о правых Эсерах).** In: *Правда,* no. 29, Feb. 8, 1919, p. 1.

234 **Откровенность Колчака.** In: *Правда,* no. 176, Aug. 10, 1919, p. 1.

235 **Памяти Карла Либкнехта и Розы Люксембург. Сборник статей,** by Bukharin *et al.* Москва, Советский мир, 1919. 63 p.

NNC RZIA

Bukharin's contribution includes: Неукротимый вождь; Памяти товарища Либкнехта (see also no. 225). Социал-демократы, которые зарезали Либкнехта и Люксембург (see also no. 262).

Other editions:
Петроград, n. p., 1919.

236 **Платформа Коммунистического Интернационала,** by N. Bukharin and Max Albert. In: *Коммунистический Интернационал в документах.* 2 vols.; ed., Bela Kun. Москва, Партийное изд., 1933.
NN NNC

This early draft of a program for the Communist International was later revised three times and culminated in the draft version adopted by the Comintern at its Sixth Congress in 1928. See nos. 398, 525, and 824 for subsequent versions of the draft program.

Also in:
. . . *Первый конгресс Коминтерна.* See no. 257.
Der 1. Kongress der Kommunistischen Internationale; Protokoll. Hamburg, n. p., 1920.

237 **Подготовка государственных посевов.** In: *Правда,* no. 24, Feb. 2, 1919, p. 1.

238 **Подлость и глупость.** In: *Правда,* no. 15, Jan. 22, 1919, p. 1.

239 **Политическая экономия рантье. Теория ценности и прибыли Австрийской школы.** Москва, Редакционно-Издательский отдел ВНСХ, 1919, 203 p.
NN NNC CSt-H DLC

This study was begun in 1912-13 but was not published until 1919.

Other editions:
Москва, Гос. изд., 1924. 191 p. *DLC IU UL-H*
Москва—Ленинград, n. p., 1925. 191 p.

Die politische Ökonomie des Rentners; die Wert- und Profit-theorie der österreichischen Schule. Übersetzung von Anna Lifschitz. Wien—Berlin, Verlag für Literatur und Politik, 1926. 194 p. *NNC MH IU WaU*
Wien—Berlin, Verlag für Literatur und Politik, 1926. 200 p. *CSt-H CLU ICU IU*
Wien—Berlin, n. p., 1932. 200 p.

German editions also available at *UFU OFU-R OFU-W OFU-S*

The Economic Theory of the Leisure Class. New York, International Publishers, 1927. 220 p. *NNC MH CtY NjP CLU ICU IU InU OCl WaU BS*
London, Martin Lawrence, 1927. 220 p. *NNC CU ICU*
New York, n. p., 1930.

240 **Политические мошенники.** In: *Правда,* no. 202, Sept. 12, 1919, p. 1.

241 **Признания откровенного буржуа.** In: *Правда,* no. 257, Nov. 16, 1919, p. 1.

241a Program komunistów . . . (1918). See no. 167.

242 Program of the Communists. (1918). See no. 167.

243 Програма комуністів . . . (1918). See no. 167.

244 Das Programm der Bolschewiki . . . (1918). See no. 167.

245 Programm der Kommunisten . . . (1918). See no. 167.

246 Программа и устав РКП . . .

Contains material relating to 1919 but not published until 1924. See no. 526.

247 Программа коммунистов . . . (1918). See no. 167.

248 Le programme des communistes . . . (1918). See no. 167.

249 Programme of the Communists . . . (1918). See no. 167.

250 Пути и повороты. In: *Правда,* no. 92, May 1, 1919, p. 1.

251 Рабочая аристократия или сплочение рабочих масс? In: *Правда,* no. 204, Sept. 14, 1919, p. 2.

252 Работница, к тебе наше слово! С приложением лозунгов. Москва, Гос. изд. 1919. 15 p.
NN NNC DLC CSt-H BDIC

Other editions:
Ростов-на-Дону, n. p., 1920. 15 p.
Казань, n. p., 1920. 15 p.
Иркутск, n. p., 1920. 15 p.

253 **Развал старой Европы.** In: *Правда,* no. 274, Dec. 6, 1919, p. 1.

254 **Речь о партийной программе...**

This speech at the Eighth Congress of the Russian Communist Party was delivered in 1919 (see no. 255 for a complete record of Bukharin's remarks to the Congress), but it was published separately in 1920. See no. 324.

255 **[Remarks of Bukharin.]** In: *VIII съезд Российской Коммунистической партии (большевиков). Стенографический отчет.* Москва—Ленинград, Коммунист, 1919, 415 p.

Available in various libraries.

256 **[Remarks of Bukharin.]** In: *Четвертый Всероссийский съезд Советов рабочих, крестьянских, солдатских и казачьих депутатов. Стенографический отчет.* Москва, Гос. изд., 1919. 442 p.

257 **[Remarks of Bukharin.]** In: *Протоколы конгрессов Коммунистического Интернационала. Первый конгресс Коминтерна.* Москва, Партийное изд., 1933. 275 p.

NN

258 **[Remarks of Bukharin.]** In: *Второй Всероссийский съезд профессиональных союзов. Стенографический отчет.* Москва, Гос. изд., 1921. 196 p.

NN

259 **Роза Люксембург и правительство Учредительного собрания.** In: *Правда,* no. 126, June 13, 1919, p. 1.

260 **Рыцари духа.** In: *Правда,* no. 185, Aug. 22, 1919, p. 1.

261 **Смерть Гаазе.** In: *Правда,* no. 252, Nov. 11, 1919, p. 1.

262 **Социал-демократы, которые зарезали Либкнехта и Люксембург.** In: *Правда,* no, 12, Jan. 18, 1919, p. 1.

Also in:
Памяти Карла Либкнехта и Розы Люксембург ... See no. 235.

263 **«Свободолюбивые» убийцы.** In: *Правда,* no. 5, Jan. 10, 1919, p. 1.

264 **Текущая задача.** In: *Правда,* no. 143, July 3, 1919, p. 1.

265 **Теория пролетарской диктатуры.** In: *Октябрьский переворот и диктатура пролетариата. Сборник статей.* Москва, Гос. изд., 1919. 324 p.
NN NNC CSt-H

Other editions:
Диктатура пролетариата. New York, Федерация русских отделов коммунистической рабочей партии в Америке, 1920. 31 p. *NN NNC MH NjP*
Диктатура пролетариятй. New York, Видання Української федерації комуністичної партії в Америці, 192-? 16 p. *NN*

Also in:
Атака ... See no. 460.

266 **Тибор Самуели.** In: *Коммунистический Интернационал,* no. 5, 1919, p. 711.

Also in:
Tibor Szamuely. In: *Die Kommunistische Internationale,* no. 4/5, 1919, pp. 137—138.

267 **Товарищ Ионов (Степан).** In: *Правда,* no. 88, Apr. 26, 1919, p. 1.

268 **Товарищ Свердлов.** In: *Правда,* no. 59, Mar. 1919, p. 1.

269 **Трудовое добровольчество.** In: *Правда,* no. 193, Aug. 31, 1919, p. 1.

270 **Церковь и школа в советской республике...** (1918). See no. 185.

271 **Världsrevolutionens program...** (1918). See no. 167.

272 **Великое завоевание.** In: *Правда,* no. 255, Nov. 14, 1919, p. 1.

273 **Vilaggazdasag es imperialismus . . .** (1917). See no. 82.

274 **Вниманию интеллигенции.** In: *Правда,* no. 253, Nov. 12, 1919, p. 1.

275 **Vom Sturze des Zarismus bis zum Sturze der Bourgeoisie.** (1918). See no. 161.

276 **Von der Diktatur des Imperialismus zur Diktatur des Proletariats.** (1918). See no. 160.

277 **Всеобщая дележка или коммунистическое производство?** (1918). See no. 187.

1920

278 **Das ABC des Kommunismus . . .** (1919). See no. 194.

279 **Anarchismus und wissenschaftlicher Kommunismus . . .** (1918). See no. 125.

280 **Авангард международной революции.** In: *Вестник 2-го Конгресса Коммунистического Интернационала,* no. 4, Aug. 3, 1920, p. 1.

This journal was issued as a supplement to the daily issues of *Правда*. See *Правда*, no. 169, Aug. 3, 1920, for the issue indicated above. See no. 326 for a complete record of Bukharin's remarks to the Second Congress of the Comintern.

281 **Азбука коммунизма . . .** (1919). See no. 194.

282 **Азбука комунізма . . .** (1919). See no. 194.

283 **Де справжня свобода? (1919).** See no. 203.

284 **Деньги в эпохе пролетарской диктатуры.** Москва, n. p., 1920.

285 **Dies ist der letzte entscheidende Kampf.** In: *Russische Korrespondenz,* I, Bd. 1, no. 10, July, 1920, p. 102.

286 **Диктатура пролетариата.** (1919). See no. 265.

287 **The Economic Situation.** In: *Soviet Russia,* III, Aug. 7, 1920, pp. 129–144.

288 **Экономика переходного периода. Часть I: Общая теория трансформационного процесса.** Москва, Гос. изд., 1920. 157 p.

NN NNC CSt-H DLC RZIA

Part II of this controversial book was not published. Shortly after its publication, Bukharin abandoned its radical and extreme views which reflected the last echo of his "leftist" position.

Other editions:

Ökonomik der Transformatiosperiode; Autorisierte Übertragung aus dem Russischen von Frieda Rubiner. Hamburg, Verlag der Kommunistischen Internationale. Auslieferungstelle für Deutschland C. Hoym Nachfolger L. Cahnbley, 1922. 199 p.

NN NNC MH CU CLU ICU InU UFU

Ylimenokauden Taloustiede 1 Osa. Transformatsiooniprosessin Yleien Teoria. Pietari, n. p., 1921. 168 p.

289 **Элементарная задача в области производства коммунистов.** In: *Правда,* no. 218, Oct. 1, 1920, p. 1.

290 **Эпоха великих работ.** In: *Правда,* no. 290, Dec. 24, 1920, p. 1.

Also in:

The Epoch of Great Tasks. In: *Soviet Russia,* IV, no. 8, Feb. 19, 1921, p. 190.

291 **Die "Friedensliebe" der Entente und die der Polen.** In: *Russische Korrespondenz,* I, Bd. 1, no. 10, July, 1920, p. 104.

292 **Где настоящая свобода?** (1919). See no. 203.

293 **Готовьтесь к смотру!** In: *Правда,* no. 142, July 1, 1920, p. 1.

294 **Hol az Igazi Igazság?** by Bukharin and Endre Rudnyánszky. Moscow, n. p., 1920. 13 p.

295 **К комунизму через диктатуру пролетариата.** Смоленск, ЦК КПЛ и Б., 1920. 8 p.

RZIA

Other editions:
Киев—Одесса, Коммунист, 1920. 8 p.

296 **К открытию Всероссийского Союза Молодежи (РКСМ).** In: *Правда,* no. 220, Oct. 30, 1922, p. 1.

297 **К постановке производственной пропаганды.** In: *Производственная пропаганда. Сборник ...* See no. 322.

298 **К приезду тов. Бела Куна. Привет старому другу.** In: *Правда,* no. 179, Aug. 14, 1920, p. 1.

299 **Карл Либкнехт и рабочая молодежь.** In: *Правда,* no. 11, Jan. 17, 1920, p. 2.

300 **Der Klassenkampf und die Revolution in Russland.** (1917). See no. 68.

301 **Классовая борьба и революция в России.** (1917). See no. 68.

302 **Ко всем работницам.** In: *Правда,* no. 116, May 30, 1920, p. 2.

303 **Kommunismus Abécése ...** (1919). See no. 194.

304 **Komunisma Abeze ...** (1919). See no. 194.

305 **Меньшевики за сытого против голодного.** In: *Правда,* no. 40, Feb. 22, 1920, p. 1.

306 **Мистицизм и интеллигенция.** In: *Правда,* no. 145, July 4, 1920, pp. 1–2.

307 **На фронте и в тылу.** In: *Правда,* no. 7, Jan. 13, 1920, p. 1.

308 **На повороте.** In: *Правда,* no. 36, Feb. 18, 1920, p. 1.

309 **Новое в русской революции.** In: *Правда,* no. 250, Nov. 7, 1920, pp. 3–4.

Also in:
Третья годовщина Великого Октября 1917—1920. Баку, n. p., 1920.
Das Neue in der Russischen Revolution. In: *Russische Korrespondenz,* I, Bd. 2, no. 19/20, Dec., 1920, pp. 1122—1124.
What is New in the Russian Revolution. In: *Soviet Russia,* IV, no. 7, Feb. 12, 1921, pp. 153-176.

310 **О наступительной тактике.** In: *Коммунистический Интернационал,* II, no. 15, 1920, pp. 3073–3075.

Also in:
Über die Offensivtaktik. In: *Die Kommunistische Internationale,* II, no. 15, 1920, pp. 67-71.

311 **О производственной пропаганде и агитации.** N. p., n. p., 1920?

312 **О Рижских переговорах.** In: *Коммунистический Интернационал,* II, no. 15, 1920.

312a **Об экономических особенностях переходного периода.** In. *Еженедельник Правды,* no. 14, Nov. 20, 1920?

313 **Парламентарная или советская республика.** N. p., n. p., 1920?

Other editions:
Soviets or Parliaments? London, Worker's Socialist Federation, 192-? 7 p.
NNC MH CtY NjP OFU-W

314 **Положение о работе бюро производственной пропаганды.** In: *Производственная пропаганда. Сборник . . .* See no. 322.

315 **Праздник или будни.** In: *Коммунистический Интернационал,* II, no. 10, 1920, pp. 1687–1688.

Also in:
A Raevskii, *История первого мая в России.* 2-е изд. Москва—Ленинград, n. p., 1924.
Feiertag oder Werktag. In: *Die Kommunistische Internationale,* II, no. 10, 1920, pp. 270-272.
Feiertag oder Werktag. In: *Russische Korrespondenz,* I, Bd. 1, no. 8/9, June. 1920, pp. 63-64.

316 **Program komunistów . . .** (1918). See no. 167.

317 **Il Programma dei Communisti . . .** (1918). See no. 167.

318 **Программа коммунистов . . .** (1918). See no. 167.

319 **Programme of the World Revolution.** (1918). See no. 167.

320 **Производственная пропаганда. Проект тезисов Главполитпросвета.** In: *Производственная пропаганда. Сборник . . .* See no. 322.

321 **Производственная пропаганда. Речь на Московской губернской конференции.** Москва, Гос. изд., 1920. 14 p.
NNC CSt-H DLC BDIC BrM RZIA

322 **Производственная пропаганда. Сборник под редакцией Е. Григорука,** by Bukharin *et al.* Киев, n. p., 1920.

Bukharin's contribution to this volume includes: К постановке производственной пропаганды. Положение о работе бюро производственной пропаганды. Производственная пропаганда. Проект тезисов Главполитпросвета. Задачи производственной пропаганды и агитации.

323 Работница, к тебе наше слово . . . (1919). See no. 252.

324 Речь о партийной программе на VIII Всероссийской съезде Коммунистической партии (большевиков); 18—23 марта 1919. Владивосток, Дальневосточный Краевой комитет Российской Коммунистической Партии (большевиков), 1920. 15 p.

CSt-H

See no. 255 for a complete record of Bukharin's remarks to the Eighth Congress of the Russian Communist Party, 1919.

325 [Remarks of Bukharin at the Third Congress of Trade Unions.] In: *Russische Korrespondenz,* I, Bd. 1, no. 6/7, Apr.—May, 1920, pp. 17—18.

See no. 328 for a complete record of Bukharin's remarks to the Congress.

326 [Remarks of Bukharin.] In: *Протоколы конгрессов Коммунистического Интернационала. Второй Конгресс коминтерна.* Москва, Партийное изд., 1934. 754 p.

Available in various libraries.

327 [Remarks of Bukharin.] In: *Протоколы съездов и конференций Всесоюзной Коммунистической партии (б). Девятый съезд РКП(б).* Москва, Партийное изд., 1934. 612 p.

Available in various libraries.

328 [Remarks of Bukharin.] In: *Третий Всероссийский съезд профессиональных союзов. Стенографический отчет.* Москва, Гос. изд., 1921. 146 p.

NN

329 [Remarks of Bukharin.] In: *Третий Всероссийский съезд РКСМ. Стенографический отчет.* Москва—Ленинград, Молодая гвардия, 1926. 325 p.

NN

330 Революционный быт. In: *Вестник 2-го Конгресса Коммунистического Интернационала,* no. 1, July 27, 1920, p. 1.

This journal was published as a supplement to the daily issues of *Правда*. See *Правда*, no. 164, July 27, 1920, for the issue indicated above; see no. 326 for a complete record of Bukharin's remarks to the Second Congress of the Comintern.

331 **Die revolutionäre Arbeitsarmee.** In: *Russische Korrespondenz,* I, Bd. 1, no. 5, Mar., 1920, p. 24.

332 **Russian "Bolshevism" and the Working Women.** In: *Soviet Russia,* III, no. 5, July 31, 1920, pp. 105–128.

333 **Съезд совхозов.** In: *Правда,* no. 14, Jan. 22, 1920, p. 1.

334 **Советский муровейник.** In: *Правда,* no. 106, May 18, 1920, p. 2.

335 **Сырьевые, топливные и продовольственные склады.** In: *Правда,* no. 32, Feb. 13, 1920, p. 1.

336 **Текущий момент.** N. p., n. p., 1920?

337 **Тов. Ленин как революционный теоретик.** In: *Правда,* no. 86, Apr. 23, 1920, p. 1.

Also in:

Ленин как революционный теоретик. In: *Ленин, 1870—1924, Сборник.* Харьков, «Путь просвещения,» 1924. 108 p. *RZIA*

Lenin als Theoretiker der Revolution. In: *Russische Korrespondenz,* I, Bd. 1, no. 8/9, June, 1920, pp. 28—31.

338 **Тов. М. П. Янышев.** In: *Правда,* no. 153, July 14, 1920, p. 2.

339 **Труд прежде и труд теперь.** In: *Трудовая повинность и задачи работниц и крестьянок,* by Bukharin *et al.* Москва, Гос. изд., 1920. 24 p. *NN*

340 **Трудовые армии и производительность труда.** In: *Правда,* no. 38, Feb. 20, 1920, p. 1.

341 **Церковь и школа в советской республике...** (1918). See no. 185.

342 **Unser Lage an der Arbeitsfront.** In: *Russische Korrespondenz,* I, Bd. 1, no. 10, July, 1920, p. 106.

343 **В. Н. Побельский.** In: *Правда,* no. 43, Feb. 26, 1920, p. 1.

344 **В поисках пути.** In: *Правда,* no. 5, Jan. 10, 1920, p. 1.

345 **Визволення народів.** In: *Національне питання і комунізм.* Відень—Львів, Комуністична бібліотека, 1920.

NNC BDIC

346 **Задачи производственной пропаганды и агитации.** In: *Производственная пропаганда. Сборник* ... See no. 322.

1921

347 **l'ABC del comunismo.** (1919). See no. 194.

348 **Das ABC des Kommunismus...** (1919). See no. 194.

349 **The ABC of Communism...** (1919). See no. 194.

350 **Азбука коммунизма...** (1919). See no. 194.

351 **Экономический базис пролетарской революции. К вопросу о революционных перспективах.** In: *Коммунист,* no. 12/13, Nov.–Dec., 1921.

Also in:
Коммунистический Интернационал. Сборник статей, by Bukharin *et al.* Казань, n. p., 1922.

352 **The Epoch of Great Tasks.** (1920). See no. 290.

353 **Гром не грянет, мужик не перекрестится.** In: *Правда,* no. 33, Feb. 15, 1921, p. 1.

353a **Интеллигенция на западе.** In: *Правда,* no. 10, Jan. 16, 1921, p. 1.

354 **Из речи т. Н. И. Бухарина на вечере воспоминаний в 1921 г.**

A speech delivered in 1921, but not published until 1922. See no. 388.

355 **Кавалерийский рейд и тяжелая артиллерия,** by N. Bukharin and G. Piatakov. In: *Красная новь,* no. 1, 1921, pp. 256–274.

This article was a defense of Bukharin's controversial *Экономика переходного периода,* published the preceding year. See no. 288.

356 **Klasse, Partei, Führer.** In: *Internationale,* IV, no. 22, 1921, pp. 496–499.

This article is an excerpt from Bukharin's *Теория исторического материализма.* See no. 377.

357 **Kommunismin Aapinen . . .** (1919). See no. 194.

358 **Наше хозяйственное строительство и задачи партии.** In: *Экономический сборник,* no. 1, 1921.

359 **Настоящая потеха и настоящее мучение!** In: *Красная новь,* no. 2, 1921, pp. 313–320.

360 **The New Economic Policy of Soviet Russia.** In: *The New Policies of Soviet Russia,* by N. Bukharin, N. Lenin, and S. J. Rutgers. Chicago, Charles H. Kerr, 1921. 127 p.

NN NNC CtY CU OCl ICU IU InU WaU

A speech to a meeting of delegates to the Third Comintern Congress delivered on July 8, 1921. There is no known Russian publication of this speech.

361 **Новая экономическая политика и профессыональные союзы.** In: *Вестник агитации и пропаганды,* no. 1, 1921.

362 **Новый курс экономической политики.** Петроград, Гос. изд., 1921. 15 p.

NN CSt-H

Other editions:
Томск, n. p., 1921. 16 p.

Also in:
Новая экономическая политика. Сборник материалов к курсам. Казань, n. p., 1921.
Экономический сборник, no. 1, 1921.
Die Neuorientierung in der ökonomischen Politik. In: *Russische Korrespondenz,* II, Bd. 2, no. 7/9, July—Oct., 1921, pp. 671—676.

363 **Новый курс экономической политики. Восстановление народного хозяйства,** by Bukharin *et al.* Ростов-на-Дону, n. p., 1921. 90 p.

Contents and location of this item are unknown.

364 **О роле профессиональных союзов в производстве,** by Bukharin *et al.* N. p., n. p., 1921.

A collection of speeches on the role of the trade unions in the USSR delivered on December 20, 1921, to a group of delegates to the Eighth All-Russian Congress of Soviets. Contents and location are unknown.

365 **О задачах и структуре профсоюзов,** by Bukharin *et al.* In: *Правда,* no. 10, Jan. 16, 1921, pp. 2—3.

Other editions:
О задачах и структуре профсоюзов, by Bukharin *et al.* Москва, Гос. изд., 1921. 14 p. *BrM*

366 **От крушения царизма до падения буржуазии.** (1918). See no. 161.

367 **Партия рабочего класса.** In: *Правда,* no. 190, Aug. 28, 1921, p. 3.

Also in:

Новая экономическая политика. Сборник материалов к курсам. Казань, n. p., 1921.

Die Partei der Arbeiterklasse. In: *Russische Korrespondenz,* II, Bd. 2, no. 7/9, July—Oct., 1921, pp. 795—799.

368 **Подрастающие резервы и коммунистическое воспитание.** In: *Коммунистический путь,* no. 7, Dec., 1921.

369 **Польская провокация.** In: *Правда,* no. 89, Apr. 27, 1921, p. 1.

370 **Программа коммунистов . . .** (1918). See no. 167.

371 **[Remarks of Bukharin.]** In: *1-ый Международный конгресс революционных профессиональных и производственных союзов. Стенографический отчет.* Москва, Печатное бюро конгресса, 1921. (17 bulletins.)

NN

372 **[Remarks of Bukharin.]** In: *Четвертый Всероссийский съезд профессиональных союзов. Стенографический отчет.* Москва, Изд. РИОВ ЦСПС, 1922. 247 p.

NN

373 **[Remarks of Bukharin.]** In: *Protokoll des III Kongresses der Kommunistischen Internationale.* Hamburg, C. Hoym Nachfolger, 1921. 1086 p.

NN

An original Russian edition of the minutes of the Third Comintern Congress could not be located.

374 **[Remarks of Bukharin.]** In: *Протоколы съездов и конференций Всесоюзной Коммунистической Партии (б). Десятый съезд РКП (б).* Москва, Партийное Изд., 1933. 954 p.

NN NNC

375 **[Remarks of Bukharin.]** In: *Всероссийская конференция РКП (большевиков). Бюллетень № 1—5.* Москва, n. p., 1921.

NN

376 **Синдикализм и коммунизм (По поводу фельетона Ленина).** In: *Правда,* no. 15, Jan. 25, 1921, p. 1.

377 **Теория исторического материализма. Популярный учебник марксистской социологии.** Москва, Гос. изд., 1921. 383 p.

DS OFU-R CSt-H

This was Bukharin's most complete statement of his distinctive and controversial theory of dialectical and historical materialism.

Other editions:

Москва, Гос. изд., 1922. 307 p. *NNC CSt-H*
Нижний Новгород, n. p., 1922. 307 p.
Курск, n. p., 1922. 335 p.
Москва—Петроград, Гос. изд., 1923. 383 p.
Москва—Петроград, Гос. изд., 1923. 332 p. *NN NNC MH CtY NjP IU WaU*
Симферополь, n. p., 1923. 323 p.
Симферополь, n. p., 1923. 327 p.
Москва—Петроград, Гос. изд., 1924. 390 p. (С приложением статьи «К постановке проблем теории исторического материализма». See no. 420).
CSt-H InU
Киев, n. p., 1925, 287 p.
Москва—Ленинград, Гос. изд., 1925. 390 p.
Москва—Ленинград, Гос. изд., 1928. 390 p.
Москва—Ленинград, Гос. изд., 1928. 390 p.
Москва—Ленинград, Гос. изд., 1929. 390 p. (С приложением статьи «К постановке проблем теории исторического материализма». See no. 420.)
NNC DLC
Москва—Ленинград, Гос. изд., 1929. 390 p. (Т. же)
Москва—Ленинград, Гос. изд., 1929. 390 p. (Т. же)

Теорія історичного матеріялізму. Популярний підручник марксистської соціології. Авторизований переклад М. Ільтичої. Берлін, Укр.-Амер. вид-во Космос, 1923. 325 p. *MH InU*

Theorie des historischen Materialismus. Gemeinverständliches Lehrbuch der marxistischen Soziologie. Hamburg, Verlag der Kommunistischen Internationale. Auslieferungsstelle für Deutschland, C. Hoym Nachfolger, L. Cahnbley, 1922. 372 p.
NNC MH CLU CSt-H IU ICU

La théorie du matérialisme historique. Manuel populaire de sociologie marxiste. Traduction de la 4. edition suivie d'une note sur la position du problème du matérialisme historique. Paris, Éditions Sociales Internationales, 1927. 358 p.
CtY CSt-U CLU
Paris, Impr. "Union," 1927. 359 p. *UL-H*

Historical Materialism; A System of Sociology. Authorized Translation from the Third Russian Edition. New York, International Publishers, 1925. 318 p.
NN MH DLC CtY CSt-H ICU IU InU OCl CLU WaU

New York, International Publishers, 1928. 318 p. *NNC NjP*
New York, International Publishers, 1933. 318 p. *CtY CU*
New York, International Publishers, 1934. 318 p. *MH*
London, G. Allen and Unwin, 1926. 318 p. *NNC CLU DS*

El Materialismo Historico. Traducido de la Edición Inglesa por Pablo de la Torriente Brau y Gabriel Barceló. Madrid, n. p., 1933. 382 p.
Santiago de Chile, n. p., 1938 ? 395 p.

Vesturiska Materijalizma Teorija. Populars Marksistiskas Sociologijas Kurss. No Krievu Valodas Tulkojis P. Dauge. Maskava, n. p., 1923. 288 p.

Also in:
Класс и сословие. In: *Марксистская хрестоматия*... See no. 496.
Классы. In: *Марксистская хрестоматия*... See no. 496.
Техника как основа производительных сил. In: *Марксистская хрестоматия*... See no. 496.
Klasse, Partei, Führer. In: *Internationale,* IV, no. 22, 1921, pp. 496—499.

378 Über den Parteiaufbau. Rede auf dem X. Kongress der Kommunistischen Partei Russland. Moskau, March 1921. In: *Russische Korrespondenz,* II, Bd. 1, no. 5, pp. 325–334.

For a complete record of Bukharin's remarks to the Tenth Congress of the Russian Communist Party, see no. 374.

379 What is New in the Russian Revolution. (1920). See no. 309.

380 Ylimenokauden taloustiede 1 osa... (1920). See no. 288.

1922

381 The ABC of Communism... (1919). See no. 194.

382 Anarchia e communismo scientifico. (1918). See no. 125.

383 Азбука коммунизма... (1919). See no. 194.

384 Буржуазная революция и революция пролетарская. In: *Под знаменем марксизма,* no. 7/8, July–Aug. 1922, pp. 61–82.

Also in:
Атака... See no. 460.

385 **The Economic Structure of Soviet Russia.** In: *Inpreçor,* II, no. 22, 1922.

386 **Экономический базис пролетарской революции . . .** (1921). See no. 351.

387 **Ильич.** In: *Тов. Ленин на отдыхе. Иллюстрированное приложение к № 215 «Правды,»* Sept. 24, 1924, p. 4.

388 **Из речи т. Н. И. Бухарина на вечере воспоминаний в 1921 г.** In: *Пролетарская революция,* no. 10, Oct., 1922, pp. 316–322.

Speech delivered in 1921; not published until 1922.

389 **Хозяйственные формы в Советской России.** In: *Правда,* no. 30, Feb. 8, 1922, p. 1.

390 **Коммунистическое воспитание молодежи в условиях нэпа . . .**

A speech delivered to the Fifth Komsomol Congress in 1922 (see no. 399 for full report); also published separately in 1923. See no. 422.

391 **Komunisam Aspukki . . .** (1919). See no. 194.

391a **A Kommunizmus Ábéséje . . .** (1919). See no. 194.

392 **Мировое хозяйство и империализм . . .** (1917). See no. 82.

393 **Обоснование партийной программы. Доклад на VIII съезде РКП.** 1919. In: *Программа и устав РКП (большевиков). С докладами Н. И. Бухарина и В. И. Ленина на VIII съезде партии.* Москва, n. p., 1922. *OFU-G*

This report was delivered to the Eighth Congress of the Russian Communist Party in 1919 and published in 1922, 1924, and 1925, as indicated above. See no. 255 for a complete record of Bukharin's remarks to the Congress.

Other editions:
Москва, Гос. изд., 1924. 174 p. *NN CU*
Москва, n. p., 1925.

394 Ökonomik der Transformationsperiode . . . (1920). See no. 288.

395 The Political Prisoners. In: *Inprecor,* II, nos. 32, 33, 1922.

396 Политическая экономия без ценности . . . (1913). See no. 10.

397 Проблемы распределения. In: *Основные проблемы политической экономии. Сборник статей, Под редакцией и с предисловием С. Дволайского и И. Рубина.* Москва–Ленинград, n. p., 1922.

Other editions:
Москва, n. p., 1924.

398 [Проект программы Коммунистического Интернационала.]

This draft program was written in 1922 and presumably published in Russian, but the earliest known version is an English translation in *Inprecor,* II, no. 103, 1922. It was the second such draft composed by Bukharin for consideration by the Fourth Congress of the Comintern, and it was followed by two subsequent versions, culminating in the adoption of his fourth and final draft in 1928 (see nos. 236, 525, 824).

Also in:
Спутник коммуниста, no. 19, 1923, pp. 131-148.
Towards a Communist Programme. London, n. p., 1923, pp. 23-39. *OFU-W*
Атака . . . See no. 460.

399 [Remarks of Bukharin.] In: *Пятый Всероссийский съезд РКСМ. Стенографический отчет.* Москва–Ленинград, Молодая гвардия, 1927. 380 p. *NN*

400 [Remarks of Bukharin.] In: *Процесс эсеров. Речи защитников и обвиняемых.* Москва, Красная новь, 1922. 242 p. *NNC*

401 Теория исторического материализма . . . (1921). See no. 377.

402 Theorie des historischen Materialismus . . . (1921). See no. 377.

403 Who Are the Traitors? In: *Inprecor,* II, no. 52, 1922.

404 **За пять лет,** by Bukharin *et al.* N. p., n. p., 1922? *NNC*

Bukharin's contribution includes Железная когорта революции. See no. 405.

405 **Железная когорта революции.** In: *За пять лет,* by Bukharin *et al.* N. p., n. p., 1922? *NNC*

Also in:
Die eiserne Kohorte der Revolution. In: *Russische Korrespondenz,* III, Bd. 2, no. 11/12, 1922, pp. 729-733.
Вождъ пролетариата — Российская Коммунистическая Партия. Сборник, by Bukharin *et al.* n. p., Прибой, 1923. 242 p. NNC

1923

406 **Das ABC des Kommunismus...** (1919). See no. 194.

407 **Almanach des Verlages der Kommunistischen Internationale,** by Bukharin *et al.* Hamburg, n. p., 1923.

Contents and location of this item are unknown.

408 **Anarquismo y communismo cientifico...** (1918). See no. 125.

409 **Азбука коммунизма...** (1919). See no. 194.

410 **Centralismen og det Norske Arbeiderparti.**

Written in 1923, but not published until 1924. See no. 464.

411 **Чем мы побеждаем.** In: *Вождъ пролетариата — Российская Коммунистическая Партия. Сборник,* by Bukharin *et al.* N. p., Прибой, 1923. 242 p. *NNC*

412 **Дискуссия о пролетарской культуре,** by Bukharin and [?] Jakovlev In: *Спутник коммуниста,* no. 19, 1923, pp. 95—130.

413 **Доклад. IV Всероссийский съезд работников печати.** In: *Известия,* no. 28, Feb. 8, 1923, p. 3.

414 **Доклад о международном положении.** N. p., n. p., 1923?

415 **Енчмениада. К вопросу об идеологическом вырождении.** In: *Красная новь,* no. 6 (16), 1923, pp. 145—178.

Other editions:
Енчмениада (К вопросу об идеологическом вырождении). Москва—Петроград, n. p., 1923. 72 p.
Москва, Гос. изд., 1924. 72 p. *NN DS*

Also in:
Атака . . . See no. 460.

416 **Голос миллионов. Экстренный пленум Московского совета. Речь тов. Н. И. Бухарина.** In: *Правда,* no. 105, May 13, 1923, p. 3.

417 **A Great Marxian Party.** In: *The Communist Review,* IV, no. 1, 1923.

The Russian original of this article, if originally published in Russian, is unknown.

Also in:
A Great Marxian Party. In: *Inprecor,* III, no. 29, 1923.
Eine grosse marxistische Partei. In: *Internationale Presse-Korrespondenz,* III, no. 45, 1923, pp. 338—339.

418 **The International of General, Equal, and Open Abjectness!** In: *Inprecor,* III, no. 37, 1923.

419 **Итоги XII съезда РКП.** In: *Коммунистический интернационал,* no. 25, 1923.

Also in:
Итоги съезда РКП. In: *Властъ советов,* no. 5, 1923, pp. 3—9.
Die Resultate des XII. Kongresses der Kommunistischen Partei Russlands (Bolschewiki) In: *Die Kommunistische Internationale,* IV, no. 26, 1923, pp. 26—32.
The Twelfth Congress of the Communist Party. In: *The Communist International,* no. 25, 1923.

420 **К постановке проблем теории исторического материализма (Беглые заметки).** In: *Вестник Социалистической академии,* no. 3, 1923, pp. 3–15.

This justification of Bukharin's controversial *Теория исторического материализма* published in 1921 (see no. 377), was written in response to criticism of his book and reaffirmed his views in it.

Also in:
Теория исторического материализма. Москва, Гос. изд., 1924, [appendix] pp. 359—371. See no. 377.
Москра—Ленинград, Гос. изд., 1929. 390 p.
La théorie du matérialisme ... See no. 377.
Атака ... See no. 460.

421 **Класова боротьба й революція в Росії.** (1917). See no. 68.

422 **Коммунистическое воспитание молодежи в условиях нэпа. Доклад на 5 Всероссийском съезде РКСМ 13 сентября 1922 года.** Екатеринбург, n. p., 1923. 51 p. *ICU*

Speech delivered in 1922 but not published until 1923. For Bukharin's remarks to the Fifth Congress of the Komsomol, see no. 399.

423 **Крестьянство и рабочий класс в ближайший исторический период.** In: *Правда,* no. 219, Sept. 26, 1923, p. 1.

Also in:
N. Lenin, *Пролетариат и крестъянство.* Харьков, «Пролетарий,» 1924. 130 p.
The Peasantry and the Working Class in the Next Historical Period. In: *Inprecor,* III, no. 67, 1923.

424 **Критика и критика.** In: *Правда,* no. 144, June 30, 1923, p. 1.

425 **Кризис капитализма и коммунистическое движение.** Москва, Красная новь, 1923. 83 p. *NNC*

This is a reprint of a speech delivered to the Twelfth Congress of the Russian Communist Party in April 1923. (See no. 446 for Bukharin's remarks to the Congress.)

426 **Культурный фронт и интеллигентский пессимизм.** In: *Правда,* no. 139, June 24, 1923, p. 1.

427 **The Limits of Centralism in the Comintern.** In: *Inprecor,* III, nos. 46, 49, 1923.

A speech delivered to the Third Enlarged Plenum of the Executive Committee of the Comintern. (See no. 445 for a full report of Bukharin's remarks to the meeting.)

428 **Международная политика пролетарского государства.** In: *Правда,* no. 6, Jan. 11, 1923, p. 3.

Also in:
The International Policy of the Proletarian State. In: *Inprecor,* III, no. 10, 1923.

429 **Мировое хозяйство и империализм...** (1917). See no. 82.

430 **Myj-ponda me loi kommunistka. Roč kylys' lösödis N. P. Čensov.** N. p., n. p., 1923. *DS*

431 **На посту. Юбилейный журнал Харьковской губернской рабоче-крестьянской милиции и отдела управления губисполкома,** by Bukharin *et al.* Харьков, n. p., 1923.

Contents and location of this item are unknown.

432 **Основные итоги XII съезда РКП. С приложением резолюции съезда,** by Bukharin and G. Zinoviev. Краснодар, Буревестник, 1923. 143 p.

433 **От крушения царизма до падения буржуазии.** (1918). See no. 161.

434 **Первая ласточка.** In: *Правда,* no. 7, Jan. 12, 1923, p. 1.

435 **Письмо тов. Бухарина тов. Суварину.** In: *Известия,* no. 6, June 11, 1923, p. 3.

436 **Письмо тт. Бухарина и Зиновьева министру юстиции Франции.** In: *Правда,* no. 35, Feb. 16, 1923, p. 1.

437 По поводу порядка дня партийного съезда. In: *Правда,* no. 16, Jan. 25, 1923, p. 1.

438 По скучной дороге (Ответ моим критикам). In: *Красная новь,* no. 1 (11), 1923, pp. 273—289.

This article was the first of seven planned sections of a response to critics of Bukharin's philosophical views. The other six installments were never published.

439 Политическая экономия рантье... (1919). See no. 239.

440 Проект программы Коммунистического Интернационала. (1922). See no. 398.

441 The Program Question. In: *Inprecor,* III, no. 49, 1923.

442 Das Programm der Kommunistischen Internationale und ihrer einzelnen Parteien. In: *Bericht über den 4. Kongress der Kommunistischen Internationale,* Hamburg, n. p., 1923, pp. 100–105.

443 Пролетарская революция и культура. Петроград, «Прибой,» 1923. 56 p. *NNC CSt-H BrM Inl*

Other editions:

Петроград, «Прибой», 1925. 56 p. *NNC*

Proletarische Revolution und Kultur. Vortrag, gehalten am 3. Februar 1923 in Petrograd. Hamburg, C. Hoym Nachfolger, 1923. 82 p. *CSt-H DS BS BHW*

444 Развитие капитализма и его гибель... (1919). See no. 194.

445 [Remarks of Bukharin.] In: *III Расширенный пенум Исполнительного Комитета Комунистического Интернационала. Отчет.* Москва, Красная новь, 1923, 320 p. *Available in various libraries.*

446 **[Remarks of Bukharin.]** In: *Двенадцатый съезд Российской Коммунистической Партии (большевиков). Стенографический отчет.* Москва, Красная новь, 1923. 705 p. *Available in various libraries.*

447 **[Remarks of Bukharin.]** In: *Protokoll des vierten Kongresses der Kommunistischen Internationale.* Hamburg, Carl Hoym Nachfolger, 1923. 1086 p.

Available in various libraries. An original Russian edition of the minutes of the Fourth Comintern Congress could not be located.

448 **Die Ruhr Besetzung und Sowjetrussland.** In: *Internationale Presse-Korrespondenz,* III, no. 31, 1923, pp. 229–230.

449 **Speeches of Bukharin and Thalheimer on the Programme of the Communist International at the Fourth Congress.** In: *Towards a Communist Programme.* London, n. p., 1923, pp. 5–22. *OFU-W*

For a complete account of Bukharin's remarks to the Fourth Congress of the Comintern, see no. 447.

449a **Теоретик рабочего класса.** In: *Звезда,* V, no. 17, 1923?

450 **Теория исторического материализма . . .** (1921). See no. 377.

451 **Теорія історичного матеріялізму . . .** (1921). See no. 377.

452 **Vesturiska Materijalizma Teorija . . .** (1921). See no. 377.

453 **Влияние нэпа и «уклоны» в рабочем движении.** In: *Правда,* no. 60, Mar. 25, 1923, p. 2.

454 **Вопросы первого всесоюзного совещания рабкоров.** In: *О рабкоре и селькоре . . .* See no. 698.

455 Вождь пролетариата — Российская Коммунистическая Партия. Сборник, by Bukharin *et al.* N. p., Прибой, 1923. 242 p. *NNC*

Bukharin's contribution includes: Чем мы побеждаем? Желездая когорта революции (1922).

456 Железная когорта революции (1922). In: *Вождь пролетариата . . .* See no. 455; see also main entry, no. 405.

1924

457 ABC of Communism . . . (1919). See no. 194.

458 Анархия мирового хозяйства. In: *Марксистская хрестоматия . . .* See no. 496.

An excerpt from *Мировое хозяйство и империализм . . .* See no. 82.

459 Dem Andenken. In: *Lenin: Leben und Werk . . .* See no. 490.

460 Атака. Сборник теоретических статей. Москва, Гос. изд., 1924. 303 p. *NN NNC MH DLC CSt-H CtY CU UL-H*

Contents. — Буржуазная революция и революция пролетарская (1922). — Енчмениада (1923). — Фокус-покусы г-на Струве (1913). — Ленин как марксист (1924). — О мировой революции, нашей стране, культуре и прочем (1924). — Политическая экономия без ценности . . . (1913). — Проект программы Коммунистического Интернационала (1922). — Теоретическое примиренчество (1914). — Теория либерального социализма (1913). — Теория пролетарской диктатуры (1919). — Теория субъективной ценности Бем-Баверка (1914). — К постановке проблем теории исторического материализма (1923).

Other editions:
Москва, Гос. изд., 1924. 303 p.

461 Азбука коммунизма . . . (1919). See no. 194.

462 Brothers in Lenin. See no. 571.

463 Буржуазная революция и революция пролетарская (1922). In: *Атака...* See no. 460; see also main entry, no. 384.

464 Centralismen og det Norske Arbeiderparti. Andelsfore, Vest Arbeidersblat, 1924. 16 p.

Written in June 1923, but not published until 1924.

465 A Counter-Maneuver of Gompers. In: *Inprecor,* IV, no. 82, 1924.

466 Денежная реформа и с.-х. кооперация. In: *Правда,* no. 64, Mar. 20, 1924, p. 1.

467 Диктатура пролетариата и рабкоровские организации. In: *О рабкоре и селькоре...* See no. 698.

This article was written in 1924 and probably published in 1924 in a volume of which there is no record, although it is alluded to in the 1926 edition of *О рабкоре и селькоре...*

468 Доклад. V всемирный конгресс Коминтерна. Программа Коммунистического Интернационала. In: *Известия,* no. 146, June 29, 1924, p. 3; no. 147, July 1, 1924, p. 5.

For a complete record of Bukharin's remarks to the Fifth Congress of the Comintern, see no. 532; see also nos. 474 and 516b.

469 [Долой фракционность.]

The earliest known version of this item was published in German in 1924 and in Russian only in the following year.

Other editions:

Nieder mit der Fraktionsmacherei. Im Anhang L. Trotzki; Der Neue Kurs. Hamburg, C. Hoym Nachfolger, L. Cahnbley, 1924. 67 p. *NN MH CSt-H DS*

Долой фракционность! In: *К вопросу о троцкизме. Сборник статей.* Москва—Ленинград, Гос. изд., 1925. 192 p. *NN MH CSt-H DLC InU UL-H*

Also in:

Nieder mit der Fraktionsmacherei. In: *Internationale,* VII, no. 7/8, 1924. (Supplement, 28 p.)

470 **Два слова о некоторых особенностях рабкоровской работы.** In: *О рабкоре и селькоре...* See no. 698.

This article was written in April 1924 and probably published in 1924 in a preceding version of the 1926 edition of *О рабкоре и селькоре...* There is no record of the earlier edition, however, other than an allusion to it in the later edition.

471 **Единственный — неповторяемый. Сборник статей, воспоминаний, стихов памяти Ленина. Под редакцией Н. Райвида и В. Касперского,** by Bukharin *et al.* Екатеринбург, n. p., 1924.

Contents and location of this item are unknown.

Other editions:
Екатеринбург, n. p., 1924.

472 **Енчмениада...** (1923) See no. 415.

Also in:
Атака... See no. 460.

473 **Эпоха империализма.** In: V. Iakovlev,, *Империалистическая война и большевики.* Иваново-Вознесенск, Основа, 1924. *NNC BDIC*

474 **Fifth Congress of the Communist International, Report on the Program Question by N. Bukharin, with a Supplementary Report by A. Thalheimer; Delivered on June 27–28, 1924.** Moscow, Press Bureau of the Fifth Congress of the Comintern, 1924. 43 p. *NN CSt-H*

For a complete record of Bukharin's remarks to the Fifth Congress of the Comintern, see no. 532; see also nos. 468 and 516b.

Other editions:
The V World Congress of the Communist International; Report of Comrades Bukharin and Thalheimer on the Program Question. In: *Inprecor,* IV, nos. 47, 50, 1924.
V Kongres der Kommunistischen Internationale; zur Programmfrage der Kommunistischen Internationale; zwei Reden, gehalten am 27. und 28. Juni 1924 von N. Bucharin und A. Thalheimer. Moskau, n. p., 1924. 44 p.
Ve Congrès de l'Internationale Communiste. Rapports sur la question du programme de l'Internationale Communiste par Boukharine et Thalheimer (27 et 28 Juin 1924). Moscou, Bureau de la Presse de l'Internationale Communiste, 1924. 39 p. *UL-H*

475 **Фокус-покусы г-на Струве.** (1913). In: *Атака...* See no. 460; see also no. 5.

476 **Genosse.** In: *Lenin: Leben und Werk . . .* See no. 490; see also no. 547.

477 **Империализм и накопление капитала.** In: *Под знаменем марксизма,* no. 8/9, 1924; no. 1/2, 3, 1925.

This work was intended by Bukharin to be a critique of Rosa Luxemburg's *Die Akkumulation des Kapitals,* a solution of the dilemma in classical Marxian theory of the doctrine of the accumulation of capital and the downfall of capitalism, and a definitive theoretical basis for the Communist International and its program, under consideration during the 1920s.

Other editions:
Империализм и накопление капитала (Теоретический этюд). Москва—Ленинград, Гос. изд., 1925, 136 р. *CtY*
Москва—Ленинград, n. p., 1926. 136 р.
Москва—Ленинград, Гос. изд., 1927. 135 р. *NN CSt-H*
Москва—Ленинград, Гос. изд., 1928. 131 р. *MH DLC*
Москва—Ленинград, Гос. изд., 1929. 131 р. *NNC DLC*

Der Imperialismus und die Akkumulation des Kapitals. Wien—Berlin, Verlag für Literatur und Politik, 1926. 127 p. *MH ICU IU InU UFU OFU-S*
Wien—Berlin, n. p., 1927. 127 p.
Wien—Berlin, n. p., 1932. 127 p.

Also in:
Der Imperialismus und die Akkumulation des Kapitals. In: *Unter dem Banner des Marxismus,* I, no. 1, 1925, pp. 21-36; no. 2, pp. 231-290.

477a **К итогам английских выборов.** In: *Правда,* no. 251, Nov. 2, 1924, p. 1.

478 **К постановке проблем теории исторического материализма . . .** (1923). In: *Теория исторического материализма . . .* See no. 377 and also no. 420.

Also in:
Атака . . . See no. 460.

479 **К вопросу о международной связи.** In: *О рабкоре и селькоре . . .* See no. 698.

This item is the record of a speech delivered by Bukharin on July 11, 1924, to a meeting of workers' correspondents and delegates to the Fifth Congress of the Comintern. It was probably published in a preceding version of the 1926 edition of *О рабкоре и селькоре . . .* There is no record of the earlier edition, however, other than an allusion to it in the later edition.

480 **К вопросу о программе Коммунистического Интернационала,** by Bukharin *et al.* Москва, n. p., 1924.

Contents and location are unknown.

481 **К вопросу об организации рабкоров и селькоров.** In: *Правда,* no. 295, Dec. 28, 1924, p. 2.

Also in:
О рабкоре и селькоре... See no. 698.

482 **Как не нужно писать историю Октября. (По поводу книги т. Троцкого «1917 г.»).** In: *Правда,* no. 251, Nov. 2, 1924, pp. 2–3.

Other editions:
Как не нужно писать историю Октября. По поводу книги тов. Троцкого «1917 г.» Москва, n. p., 1924. 16 p.

Also in:
Об «Уроках Октября». Статьи и речи. See no. 512.
К вопросу о троцкизме. Москва—Ленинград, Гос. изд., 1925. 192 p. *NN MH CSt-H DLC InU UL-H*
За ленинизм. Сборник статей. Москва—Ленинград, Гос. изд., 1925. 488 p. *NN*

483 **Как работал Ленин.** In: *Первая годовщина 1924. 21 января 1925; Ленин, о Ленине, о ленинизме,* by Bukharin *et al.* Москва, Московский рабочий, 1925. 327 p. *NN*

A speech delivered to the Sixth Congress of the Komsomol in 1924 and reprinted separately in 1925. See no. 534 for a complete record of Bukharin's remarks to the Congress.

484 **Хозяйственный рост и проблема рабоче-крестьянского блока.** In: *Большевик,* no. 14, 1924, pp. 25–35.

Also in:
Некоторые вопросы экономической политики. Сборник статей. Москва, Мосполиграф, 1925. 86 p. *NNC CSt-H DS*
Das wirtschaftliche Wachstum und das Problem des Arbeiter- und Bauernblocks. In: *Internationale,* VIII, no. 1, 1925, pp. 19—27.

485 **Класс и сословие.** In: *Марксистская хрестоматия*... See no. 496.

An except from *Теория исторического материализма*... See no. 377.

486 **Классы.** In: *Марксистская хрестоматия . . .* See no. 496.

An excerpt from *Теория исторического материализма . . .* See no. 377.

487 **Крестьянство и рабочий класс в ближайший исторический период.** (1923). See no. 423.

488 **Ленин как марксист.** In: *Вестник Коммунистической Академии,* no. 7, 1924, pp. 22–68.

A report delivered to a meeting of the Communist Academy on February 17, 1924.

Other editions:
Ленин как марксист. Харьков, Пролетарий, 1924. *CtY*
Lénine Marxiste. Paris, n. p., 1925. 50 p. *NjP UL-H*
Lenin as a Marxist. London, Communist Party of Great Britain, 1925. 64 p. *NN NNC MH CtY NjP ICU InU WaU CSt-H*

Also in:
Атака . . . See no. 460.

489 **Ленин как революционный теоретик.** (1920). See no. 337.

490 **Lenin: Leben und Werk, von N. Bucharin, J. Jaroslawski, L. Kamenov, usw.** Wien, Verlag für Literatur und Politik, 1924. 208 p. *NNC CSt-H IU InU CLU UFU*

Bukharin's contribution includes: Dem Andenken; Genosse; Der Theoretiker der Revolution.

491 **Ленин. Небольшой сборник очерков и статей о жизни и деятельности тов. Ленина,** by N. Bukharin, G. Zinoviev, and Ia. Iakovlev. Клинцы, «Труд,» 1924. 85 p.

Contains Bukharin's article, Товарищ. See no. 547.

492 **Ленин. Сборник под редакцией Д. Шафранского,** by Bukharin *et al.* Тамбов, n. p., 1924.

Contents and location of this item are unknown.

493 **Ленин — вождь Коминтерна.** In: *Красная газета,* II, no. 66, 1924?, p. 150.

A reprint of a speech delivered by Bukharin to the fourth session of the Executive Committee of the Comintern in July 1924. See no. 533 for a complete record of Bukharin's remarks to the meeting.

494 **Ленин — вождь трудящихся,** by Bukharin *et al.* Ростов-на-Дону, Прибой, 1924, 52 p.

Contents and location of this item are unknown.

495 **Ленинское воспитание молодежи. Речь на VI-ом Всесоюзном съезде Ленинского Коммунистического Союза Молодежи 15 июля 1924 г.** Москва, Молодая гвардия, 1924. 49 p.

For a complete record of Bukharin's remarks to the Sixth Congress of the Komsomol, see no. 534.

Also in:
Первая годовщина 1924. 21 января 1925. Ленин, о Ленине, о ленинизме, by Bukharin *et al.* Москва, Московский рабочий, 1925. 327 p. *NN*

496 **Марксистская хрестоматия для юношества,** compiled and edited by S. Semkovskii; by Bukharin *et al.* Москва, Гос. изд., 1924. 347 p. *NN*

Bukharin's contribution includes: Анархия мирового хозяйства; Класс и сословие; Классы; Милитаризм; Мощь трестов; От мирового капитализма к мировому социализму; Славные революции и великие бунты; Техника, как основа производительных сил. Each of these articles is an excerpt from original works by Bukharin. See the separate entries for each title in the section for the year 1924 for the source of the excerpt.

497 **Милитаризм.** In: *Марксистская хрестоматия . . .* See no. 496.

An excerpt from *Мировое хозяйство и империализм* (see no. 82).

498 **Молодняк. Доклад о работе среди молодежи на XIII съезде РКП(б). С приложением резолюции.** Екатеринбург, n. p., 1924. 34 p.

See no. 535 for a complete record of Bukharin's remarks to the Thirteenth Congress of the Russian Communist Party.

499 **Мощь трестов.** In: *Марксистская хрестоматия . . .* See no. 496.

An excerpt from *Мировое хозяйство и империализм* (see no. 82).

499a Москва в трауре... речь тов. Н. И. Бухарина. In: *Правда,* no. 22, Jan. 27, 1924, p. 3.

500 На чем нужно обучаться рабкорам. In: *О рабкоре и селькоре...* See no. 698.

This article may have been published in 1924 in a first edition of *О рабкоре и селькоре...* (1926), of which there is no record save an allusion to it in the later edition.

501 На могилу Ильича. Статьи, характеристики, воспоминания, by Bukharin *et al.* Ленинград, n. p., 1924.

Contents and location of this item are unknown.

Other editions:
Ленинград,n. p., 1924.

502 The Next Tasks of the CP in America, by Bukharin, K. Radek, and O. Kuusinen. In: R. M. Whitey, *Reds in America.* New York, Beckwith Press, 1924. 287 p. Appendix F, pp. 247–356. *NNU*

The author of this book, Whitey, presents this document as an authentic copy of a set of instructions sent to the American Communist Party by Bukharin, Radek, and Kuusinen on behalf of the headquarters of the Communist International. It contains directives concerning the preparation by American Communists for a seizure of power in the United States. The authenticity of this document remains undetermined.

502a Новое откровение о советской экономике, или как можно погубить рабоче-крестьянский блок. К вопросу об экономическом обосновании троцкизма. In: *Правда,* no. 283, Dec. 12, 1924, pp. 7–8.

A critique of Preobrazhensky's theory of "primary socialist accumulation" and a formulation of Bukharin's own approach to the problem of the transition to socialism in Russia.

Other editions:
Новое откровение о советской экономике, или как можно погубить рабоче-крестъянский блок. К вопросу об экономическом обосновании троцкизма. Москва—Ленинград, Гос. изд., 1925. 35 p. *CSt-H DLC ICU NN*

Also in:
Известия, no. 234, Dec. 12, 1924, pp. 5–6.
К вопросу о троцкизме. See no. 585.
Некоторые вопросы экономической политики... See no. 601.
За ленинизм... See no. 654.
Критика экономической платформы оппозиции. See no. 687.
A New Revelation as to Soviet Economics, or How the Workers' and Peasants' Bloc Can Be Destroyed. In: *Inprecor,* V, no. 6, 1925.

502b Новое проявление «пацифизм.» In: *Правда,* no. 274, Dec. 2, 1924, p. 1.

503 О кооперации. N.p., n.p., 1924.

504 О ликвидаторстве наших идей. In: *Большевик,* no. 2, 1924, pp. 3–9.

505 О мировой революции, нашей стране, культуре и прочем. Ответ академику Павлову. In: *Красная новь,* nos. 1, 2, 1924.

Other editions:
О мировой революции, нашей стране, культуре и прочем. Ответ академику И. Павлову. Ленинград, Гос. изд., 1924. 65 p. *MH CtY UL-H*
Ленинград, Гос. изд., 1924. 60 p. *DLC RZIA*

Also in:
Атака... See no. 460.

506 О некоторых задачах нашей работы в деревне. In: *Большевик,* no. 7/8, 1924, pp. 21–26.

507 О политике партии в художественной литературе. In: *К вопросу о политике РКП(б) в художественной литературе.* Москва, Красная новь, 1924. 109 p. *NNC*

This item is the verbatim record of Bukharin's speech to a meeting of the press section of the Central Committee of the Russian Communist Party called on May 9, 1924, to consider the party's policy toward Soviet literature.

Also in:
Вопросы культуры при диктатуре пролетариата. Сборник, by Bukharin *et al.* Москва—Ленинград, Гос. изд., 1925. 222 p. *NN*

508 О рабкоре. Сборник статей. Москва, Правда и Беднота, 1924. 50 p.

Contents and location of this item are unknown. External evidence indicates it is a preceding but not identical edition of *О рабкоре и селькоре*... (1926). See no. 698.

509 О работе среди молодежи. In: *Правда,* no. 107, May 14, 1924, p. 4.

Text of a speech by Bukharin to the Thirteenth Congress of the Russian Communist Party. See no. 535 for a complete record of his remarks to the Congress.

Other editions:
О работе молодежи. Тезисы к XIII съезду РКП(б) одобренниые ЦК. Москва, n. p., 1924. 31 p. *CtY ICU*
О работе среди молодежи. Доклад на XIII съезде РКП(б) и резолюция, принятая съездом. Баку, n. p., 1924. 50 p.
Работа среди молодежи. Доклад и резолюция XIII съезда РКП(б). Москва, n. p., 1924. 70 p.

Also in:
Партия и воспитание смены. Статьи и доклады, by N. Bukharin, G. Zinoviev, and N. K. Krupskaia. Петроград, Гос. изд., 1924. 180 p.
Ленинград, Гос. изд., 1924. 180 p.
Ленинград—Москва, Гос. изд., 1925. 180 p. *BrM BDIC RZIA DS BS*

510 О селькорах и нашей политике в деревне. In: *Правда,* no. 282, Dec. 11, 1924, p. 4.

Also in:
О рабкоре и селькоре ... See no. 698.

511 Об убийстве селькора Малиновского. In: *О рабкоре и селькоре* ... See no. 698.

This article was written in August 1924 and was probably published in that year in a preceding edition of *О рабкоре и селькоре* ... (1926). There is no record of the 1924 edition, other than an allusion to it in the later edition.

512 Об «Уроках Октября». Статьи и речи, by Bukharin *et al.* Ленинград, Прибой, 1924. 262 p.

NN

Contains Bukharin's article, Как не нужно писать историю Октября. По поводу книги т. Троцкого «1917 г.» See no. 482.

Other editions:
Об «Уроках Октября» тов. Троцкого. Сборник статей и речей тт. Сталина, Бухарина и проч. Ростов-на-Дону, Буревестник, 1925. 231 p.

513 Обоснование партийной программы ... (1919). See no. 393.

514 Общие итоги нашего развития и его перспективы. In: *Правда,* no. 243, Oct. 24, 1924, p. 5.

515 **Октябрь и дети. Воспоминания, рассказы, стихи, пьесы,** by Bukharin *et al.* Владивосток, n. p., 1924.

Contents and location of this item are unknown.

516 **От мирового капитализма к мировому социализму.** In: *Марксистская хрестоматия . . .* See no. 496.

An excerpt from *Мировое хозяйство и империализм* (see no. 82).

516a **Партия и воспоминание смены. Статьи и доклады,** by N. Bukharin, G. Zinoviev, and N. K. Krupskaia. Петроград, Гос. изд., 1924. 180 p.

Bukharin's contribution includes: О работе среди молодежи. See no. 509.

Other editions:
Ленинград, Гос. изд., 1924. 180 p.
Ленинград—Москва, Гос. изд., 1925. 180 p. *BrM BDIC RZIA DS BS*

516b **Пятый всемирный конгресс Коминтерна. Речь тов. Н. И. Бухарина.** In: *Правда,* no. 145, June 29, 1924, p. 3; no. 146, July 1, 1924, p. 3.

See nos. 468 and 474; for a complete record of Bukharin's remarks to the Fifth Congress of the Comintern, see no. 532.

517 **Письма в редакцию.** In: *Правда,* no. 2, Jan. 3, 1924, p. 5.

518 **Под знаком единства.** In: *За партию — за ленинизм.* by Bukharin *et al.* Петроград, Прибой, 1924. 216 p. *CSt-H*

519 **Политическая экономия без ценности . . . (1913).** In: *Основные проблемы политической политики . . .* See no. 10.

Also in:
Атака . . . See no. 460.

520 **Политическая экономия рантье . . .** (1919). See no. 239.

521 **Праздник или будни.** (1920). See no. 315.

522 **[Preface to] V. Sorin, Рабочая группа («Мясниковщина»).** Москва, Московский комитет Российской Коммунистической Партии, 1924. 134 p. *NN*

523 **Проблемы распределения.** (1922). See no. 397.

524 **Проект программы Коммунистического Интернационала** (1922). In: *Атака . . .* See no. 460 and no. 398.

525 **Program of the Communist International (draft submitted as a basis for discussion at the Fifth Congress of the Communist International, 1924, by N. Bukharin).** *NN CSt-H*

This item is a manuscript (typescript-duplicator copy) of a draft program distributed to members of the Fifth Congress of the Comintern. The last page (p. 34) is missing. The name "Bertram Wolfe" is written in pencil on the top of the first page. See nos. 236, 398, and 824 for other versions of the Comintern Program written by Bukharin.

526 **Программа и устав РКП (большевиков). С докладами Н. И. Бухарина и В. И. Ленина на VIII съезде партии.** (1922). See no. 393.

527 **Против рабкоровского профсоюза.** In: *О рабкоре и селькоре . . .* See no. 698.

Text of a speech by Bukharin to the Second Congress of Workers'-Peasants' Correspondents in 1924. Probably published in 1924 in a preceding edition of the 1926 edition of *О рабкоре и селькоре . . .* to which the 1926 edition alludes, but of which there is no other record.

528 **Противоречия современного капитализма.** In: *Большевик,* no. 10, 1924, pp. 7–11.

Also in:
Die Widersprüche des modernen Kapitalismus. In: *Internationale,* VII, no. 18, 1924, pp. 560—563.
Contradictions of Modern Capitalism. In: *The Communist Review,* V, no. 7, 1924.

529 **Путь к Российской Коммунистической партии (большевиков).** Актюбинск, n. p., 1924. 30 p.

530 **Речи, произнесенные на Тереке в 1924 году,** by Bukharin *et al.* Пятигорск, n. p., 1924.

Contents and location of this item are unknown.

531 **[Remarks of Bukharin.]** In: *III Конгресс красного интернационала профсоюзов. Отчет (по стенограммам).* Москва, Профинтерн, 1924. 408 p. *NN*

532 **[Remarks of Bukharin.]** In: *Пятый всемирный конгресс Коммунистического Интернационала. Стенографический отчет.* 2 vols. Москва—Ленинград, Гос. изд., 1925. *Available in various libraries.*

533 **[Remarks of Bukharin.]** In: *Расширенный пленум Исполкома (Краткий протокол).* In: *Пятый всемирный конгресс Коммунистического Интернационала. Стенографический отчет.* 2 vols. Москва—Ленинград, Гос. изд., 1925. II, pp. 5–22. *Available in various libraries.*

534 **[Remarks of Bukharin.]** In: *Шестой съезд Российского Ленинского Коммунистического Союза Молодежи. Стенографический отчет.* Москва—Ленинград, Молодая гвардия, 1924. 376. p. *NN*

535 **[Remarks of Bukharin.]** In: *Тринадцатый съезд Российской Коммунистической Партии (большевиков). Стенографический отчет.* Москва, Красная новь, 1924. 765 p. *Available in various libraries.*

536 **Революционный теоретик.** Ленинград, n. p., 1924. 12 p.

Other editions:
Ленинград, Гос. изд., 1924. 12 p. *NNC MH DLC RZIA*

Also in:
Владимир Ильич Ленин. Сборник, by Bukharin *et al.* Иваново-Вознесенск, «Основа,» 1924. 62 p.
NNC

537 Славные революции и великие бунты. In: *Марксистская хрестоматия . . .* See no. 496.

An excerpt from *От диктатуры империализма к диктатуре пролетариата.* See no. 160.

537a The Stabilization of Capitalism, the Second International, and Ourselves.

A report to the Sixth Conference of the Komsomol (see no. 534 for a full report of Bukharin's remarks to the meeting), reprinted in English translation in 1925. See no. 638.

538 «Старики» и молодежь в нашей партии. In: *За партию — за ленинизм,* by Bukharin *et al.* Петроград, Прибой, 1924. 216 p.

CSt-H

538a Статьи, характеристики, воспоминания, by Bukharin *et al.* Ленинград, «Прибой», 1924. 117 p.

Bukharin's contribution includes: Товарищ. See no. 547.

539 Техника как основа производительных сил. In: *Марксистская хрестоматия . . .* See no. 496.

An excerpt from *Теория исторического материализма . . .* See no. 377.

540 Теоретическое примиренчество. (1914). In: *Атака . . .* See no. 460.

See also main entry, no. 11.

541 Теория исторического материализма . . . (1921). See no. 377.

542 Теория либерального социализма. In: *Атака . . .* See no. 460.

Written in 1913, but not published until 1924 (see no. 9).

543 Теория перманентной революции. In: *Правда,* no. 295, Dec. 28, 1924, pp. 5—7.

Also in:

Известия, no. 296, Dec. 29, 1924, pp. 4—6.

К вопросу о троцкизме. Сборник статей. Москва—Ленинград, Гос. изд., 1925. 192 p. *NN MH CSt-H DLC InI UL-H*

За ленинизм. Сборник статей, by Bukharin *et al.* Москва—Ленинград, Гос. изд., 1925. 488 p. *NN*

О теории перманентной революции, by N. Bukharin and J. Stalin. Артемьевск, n. p., 1925. 46 p.

Über die Theorie der permanenten Revolution. In: *Um den Oktober,* by Bukharin *et al.* Hamburg, n. p., 1925. *CSt-H UFU*

Concerning the Theories of Permanent Revolution. In: *Inprecor,* V, no. 13, 1925.

544 Теория пролетарской диктатуры. (1919). In: *Атака...* See no. 460; also main entry, no. 265.

545 Теория субъективной ценности Бем-Баверка. (1914). In: *Атака...* See no. 460; also main entry, no. 12.

546 Der Theoretiker der Revolution. In: *Lenin: Leben und Werk...* See no. 490.

547 Товарищ. In: *Правда,* no. 19, Apr. 24, 1924, p. 1.

A widely circulated tribute to Lenin on the occasion of his death in 1924.

Other editions:

Товарищ. Москва, n. p., 1924.

Also in:

Статъи, характеристики, воспоминания, by Bukharin *et al.* Ленинград, «Прибой,» 1924. 117 p.

Владимир Ильич Ленин. Сборник, by Bukharin *et al.* Иваново-Вознесенск, «Основа,» 1924. 62 p. *NNC*

Ленин. Небольшой сборник очерков и статей о жизни и деятельности тов. Ленина, by N. Bukharin, G. Zinoviev, and Ia. Iakovlev. Клинцы, «Труд,» 1924. 85 p.

Первая годовщина 1924; 21 января 1925. Ленин, о Ленине, о ленинизме, by Bukharin *et al.* Москва, «Московский рабочий,» 1925. 327 p. *NN*

О Ленине. Сборник воспоминаний, by Bukharin *et al.* Москва, Гос. изд., 1925. 185 p.

Genosse. In: *Lenin: Leben und Werk,* von N. Bucharin, J. Jaroslawski, L. Kamenew, usw. Wien, Verlag für Literatur und Politik, 1924. 208 p. *NNC CSt-H CLU IU InU UFU*

548 **Товарищ Ильич. Биографии, статьи, стихи, посвященные вождю мирового пролетариата В. И. Ленину,** by Bukharin *et al.* Москва, n. p., 1924.

Contents and location of this item are unknown.

549 **Товарищ Ленин. Сборник,** by Bukharin *et al.* Москва, n. p., 1924.

Contents and location of this item are unknown.

550 **Товарищи! Умер Ленин. Мы уже никогда не увидим...** Москва, n. p., 1924. 1 p.

551 **Траурное заседание II Всесоюзного съезда советов. Речь тов. Н. И. Бухарина.** In: *Правда,* no. 22, Jan. 27, 1924, p. 3.

552 **Умер Ленин. Сборник под редакцией Бор. Волина и Мих. Кольцова,** by Bukharin *et al.* Москва, n. p., 1924.

Contents and location of this item are unknown.

553 **Уроки Английской рабочей партии.** In: *Правда,* no. 50, Mar. 1, 1924, p. 1.

554 **Владимир Ильич Ленин. Сборник,** by Bukharin *et al.* Иваново-Вознесенск, «Основа,» 1924. 62 p. ***NNC***

Bukharin's contribution includes: Революционный теоретик (see no. 536) and Товарищ (see no. 547).

555 **Вопросы жизни и борьбы. Сборник под редакцией и с предисловием Ем. Ярославского,** by Bukharin *et al.* Москва—Ленинград, Молодая гвардия, 1924.

Contents and location of this item are unknown.

556 **Вождь железной когорты. Памяти Ильича Ленина. Воспоминания, статьи, стихотворения,** by Bukharin *et al.* Ростов-на-Дону, n. p., 1924.

Contents and location of this item are unknown.

557 **Второй Интернационал под флагом «левого коммунизма.»** In: *Большевик,* no. 5/6, 1924, pp. 16—25.

558 **Второй съезд советов СССР. Речь тов. Н. И. Бухарина.** In: *Правда,* no. 23, Jan. 30, 1924, p. 6.

559 **За партию — за ленинизм,** by Bukharin *et al.* Петроград, «Прибой,» 1924. 216 p. *CSt-H*

Bukharin's contribution includes: Под знаком единства; and «Старики» и молодежь в нашей партии.

560 **Заветы Ленина и рабкоры.** In: *Рабочий корреспондент,* no. 2, 1924, pp. 6—11.

Other editions:
Заветы Ленина и рабкоры. Омск, «Рабочий путь,» 1924. 28 p.
Москва, «Правда,» 1928. 15 p.

Also in:
О рабкоре и селькоре ... See no. 698.

561 **Знамя пионеров Ленина,** by Bukharin *et al.* Москва, Молодая гвардия, 1924. 40 p.

Contents and location of this item are unknown.

1924—1925

562 **[Autobiography.]** In: *Энциклопедический словарь Русского Библиографического института Гранат.* 7th ed. 52 vols. Москва, Русский Библиографический институт Гранат, 1910—1934. Vol. 41, Part I, cols. 52—56.

Parts 1—3, vol. 41, contain biographical and autobiographical sketches of distinguished Soviet leaders, including Bukharin. Internal evidence places its writing at about 1924—1925.

563 **К критике экономической платформы оппозиции. Уроки Октября 1923 г.**

Written during late 1924 — early 1925, and not published until 1925. See no. 582.

1925

564 XIV Московская губпартконференция. Речь тов. Н. И. Бухарина. In: *Правда,* no. 282, Dec. 10, 1925, pp. 6–7.

Also in:
Речь на XIV Московской губпартконференции 6 декабря 1925 г. In: *Три речи . . .* See no. 722.
Основные черты момента. In: *Спутник коммуниста,* no. 12, 1925, pp. 8—25.

565 XIV Московская губпартконференция. Заявление тов. Н. И. Бухарина. In: *Правда,* no. 285, Dec. 13, 1925, p. 5.

566 The XIV Party Congress of the CP of Russia . . . See no. 659.

567 25-е сентября 1919 года. Памяти погибших при взрыве в Леонтьевском переупке. Сборник под редакцией Н. П. Милютиной, by Bukharin *et al.* Москва, n. p., 1925.

Contents and location of this item are unknown.

568 ABC du communisme. (1919). See no. 194.

569 Anarquismo y communismo cientifico . . . (1918). See no. 125.

570 Азбука коммунизма . . . (1919). See no. 194.

571 Brothers in Lenin. In: *The Living Age,* vol. 325, no. 4215, Apr. 18, 1925, pp. 149–154.

According to an editorial note, this item is purported to be an excerpt from a letter written by Bukharin "to an intimate friend in the opposite revolutionary camp with some doubts as to its authenticity . . . The entire 'letter,' of which approximately three-fifths is given here, has been printed privately in Berlin as a booklet under the title, "*Ibo Ia Bol'shevik.*" It has not been possible to establish the authenticity of the letter or to discover any further details concerning its background. The contents place the time of writing as 1924. It is a bitter critique of current Soviet policies and leadership, written presumably in confidence and in contradiction to Bukharin's known public position on the issues and personalities with which it deals. See his repudiation of this letter in 1928, no. 818.

572 **Concerning the Theories of Permanent Revolution.** (1924). See no. 543.

573 **Die Diktatur des Proletariats und die Klassen.** In: *Internationale,* VIII, no. 4, 1925, pp. 173–177.

574 **Диктатура пролетариата в России и мировая революция.** (1919). See no. 199.

575 **Доклад. Всесоюзное совещание с.-х. коллективов.** In: *Правда,* no. 54, Mar. 6, 1925, p. 3.

576 **Годовщина смерти Ленина,** by Bukharin *et al.* In: *Экономическая жизнь,* no. 18 (1840), Jan. 22, 1925, p. 1.

577 **Historical Materialism . . .** (1921). See no. 377.

578 **Der Imperialismus und die Akkumulation des Kapitals.** (1924). See no. 477.

579 **Империализм и накопление капитала.** (1924). See no. 477.

580 **[Introduction to] Anatolii V. Venediktov, История международного рабочего движения. Под редакцией и с предисловием Н. Бухарина. Изд. второе, исправленное и дополненное.** Москва, Гос. изд., 1925. *NN*

581 **[Introduction to] V. Sorin, Партия и оппозиция. Из истории оппозиционных течений. С предисловием Н. Бухарина.** Москва, Московский рабочий, 1925. 184 p. *NN*

582 К критике экономической платформы оппозиции. Уроки Октября 1923 г. In: *Большевик,* no. 1, 1925, pp. 25–57.

Written during the winter of 1924-1925.

Also in:
К вопросу о троцкизме ... See no. 585.
Некоторые вопросы экономической политики ... See no. 601.
Критика экономической платформы оппозиции. See no. 687.

583 К теории империалистического государства. In: *Революция права,* Москва, Коммунистическая Академия, 1925. Part I, pp. 5–32.

This item is the full text of Bukharin's article on the state, written in 1916 but not published in its entirety until 1925. When Bukharin submitted it for publication in the Bolshevik organ, *Социал-демократ,* Lenin rejected it on grounds that it contained "semi-anarchist" errors. Bukharin published the gist of the article in truncated form in several radical journals during 1916 as "Der imperialistische Raubstaat," *Jugend-Internationale* (see no. 23), "Der imperialistische Staat," *Arbeiterpolitik* (see no. 24), "De Nieuwe Lyveigenschap," *De Tribune* (see no. 29), and Новое рабство, *Новый мир* (see no. 30), as well as in *Klassekampen and Stormklockan.* Later Lenin apparently withdrew his objections to the article, for when his own statement on the theory of the state was completed less than a year afterward, it owed a large — though unacknowledged — debt to Bukharin's views, and, according to Bukharin, in a footnote added to the complete version of the article printed in 1925, Lenin conveyed through Krupskaia his agreement with Bukharin in May, 1917. See no. 26 for a reference to letters exchanged between Bukharin and Lenin concerning this dispute.

584 К вопросу о наших разногласиях ... See no. 680.

585 К вопросу о троцкизме. Москва—Ленинград, Гос. изд., 1925. 192 p.
NN MH CSt-H DLC InU UL-H

Contents — Долой фракционность! (1924) — К критике экономической платформы оппозиции (1924-1925) — Как не нужно писать историю Октября (1924) — Новое откровение о советской экономике, или как можно погубить рабоче-крестьянский блок ... (1924) — Теория перманентной революции (1924). See main entries of each of these items under the year of publication or writing indicated.

586 Как не нужно писать историю Октября ... (1924). In: *К вопросу о троцкизме.* See no. 585.

Also in:
Об «Уроках Октября» ... See no. 512.
За ленинизм ... See no. 654.
See also main entry, no. 482.

587 **Как работал Ленин.** (1924). In: *Первая годовщина 1924 . . .* See no. 622; also main entry, no. 483.

588 **Карл Либкнехт. Его жизнь и борьба. Сборник статей и материалов,** by Bukharin *et al.* Ленинград, «Молодая гвардия», 1925. 85 p.

Contents and location of this item are unknown.

589 **Хозяйственный рост и проблема рабоче-крестьянского блока.** (1924). In: *Некоторые вопросы экономической политики . . .* See no. 601; also main entry, no. 484.

590 **Коммунистическое воспитание молодежи.** Москва, Молодая гвардия, 1925. 124 p. *ICU*

591 **Комсомол, за углубленную большевистскую работу! Доклад т. Н. И. Бухарина на 9-ом губернском съезде Московской организации РЛКСМ, 23 марта 1925 г.** Москва, n. p., 1925. 32 p.

592 **Lenin As a Marxist.** (1924). See no. 488.

592a **Ленин — вождь Коминтерна.** (1924). See no. 493.

593 **Lénine marxiste.** (1924). See no. 488.

594 **Ленинская неделя в Москве. Траурное заседания ЦК, МК РКП и Института Ленина. Речь тов. Н. И. Бухарина.** In: *Правда,* no. 19, Jan. 24, 1925, p. 3.

595 **Ленинское воспитание молодежи . . .** (1924). In: *Первая годовщина 1924 . . .* See no. 622; also main entry, no. 495.

596 Meeting of the Enlarged Executive Committee of the C. I.; Report on the Discussion in the Russian Communist Party. In: *Inprecor,* V, no. 35, 1925.

See no. 634 for a complete record of Bukharin's remarks to the session; also see nos. 597, 602, and 635.

597 Meeting of the Enlarged Executive of the C. I.; Report on the Peasant Question. In: *Inprecor,* V, no. 35, 1925.

See no. 634 for a complete record of Bukharin's remarks to the session; also see nos. 596, 602, and 635.

598 Международная буржуазия и Карл Каутский — ее апостол (Ответ К. Каутскому). Москва, Изд. газеты «Правда,» 1925. 107 p. *CtY DS*

Other editions:
Москва, n. p., 1925. 107 p.

Karl Kautsky und Sowjetrussland. Eine Antwort. Wien, Verlag für Literatur und Politik, 1925. 163 p. *NN NNC MH CtY CU CSt-H UFU*
Hamburg, n. p., 1925. 163 p.
Wien, n.p., 1926. 163 p.

La bourgeoisie internationale et son apôtre Karl Kautsky (réponse à Kautsky). Paris, Librairie de l'Humanité, 1925. 124 p. *CSt-H NN IU ICU InU*
Paris, Impr. de G. Dangon, 1925. 128 p. *UL-H*

Also in:
В защиту пролетарской диктатуры. Сборник. Москва—Ленинград, Гос. изд., 1928. 260 p. *NN DLC BrM DS BS RZIA*
The International Bourgeoisie and Karl Kautsky, Its Apostle. In: *Inprecor,* V, nos. 62, 64, 65, 67, 68, 69, 70, 71, 72, 73, 1925.

599 Международное положение и задачи комсомола. In: *Правда,* no. 69, Mar. 26, 1925, p. 3.

600 Наша переписка. In: *Правда,* no. 26, Feb. 1, 1925, p. 1.

601 Некоторые вопросы экономической политики. Сборник статей. Москва, Мосполиграф, 1925. 86 p. *NNC CSt-H DS*

Contents. — Хозяйственный рост и проблема рабоче-крестьянского блока (1924) — Новое откровение о советской экономике, или как можно погубить рабоче-крестьянский блок... (1924) — К критике экономической платформы оппозиции. Уроки 1923 г. (1924—1925). See main entries of each of these items under the year of publication or writing indicated.

602 **Der neue Kurs. Reden der Genossen Bucharin und Sinowjew. Brief des EKKI.** Berlin, Vereinigung internationaler Verlags-Anstalten, 1925. 87 p. See nos. 596, 597, 635, 651, 663. *CSt-H*

602a **A New Revelation As to Soviet Economics, or How the Workers' and Peasants' Bloc Can Be Destroyed.** (1924). See no. 502a.

603 **Новое откровение о советской экономике, или как можно погубить рабоче-крестьянский блок . . .** (1924). See no. 502a.

604 **Новые задачи в области нашей крестьянской политики.** In: *Правда,* no. 94, Apr. 24, 1925, p. 1.

605 **О формальном методе в искусстве.** In: *Красная новь,* no. 3, 1925, pp. 248–257.

606 **О юных пионерах.** In: *РКП и юные пионеры.* Ленинград, «Молодая гвардия,» 1925. 34 p.

607 **О Ленине. Сборник воспоминаний,** by Bukharin *et al.* Москва, Гос. изд., 1925. 185 p.

Bukharin's contribution includes: Товарищ. See no. 547.

608 **О новой экономической политике и наших задачах.** In: *Большевик,* no. 8, 1925, pp. 3–14; no. 9/10, pp. 3–15.

Other editions:

О новой экономической политике и наших задачах. Доклад на собрании актива Московской организации 17 апреля 1925 года. Харьков, Пролетарий, 1925. 50 p. *RZIA*

609 **О политике партии в художественной литературе.** (1924). See no. 507.

610 О работе комсомола. Доклад на XIV съезде РКП(б).

This report to the Fourteenth Congress of the Russian Communist Party was delivered in December 1925 and published separately in 1926 (see no. 699). For a complete record of Bukharin's remarks to the Fourteenth Congress of the Russian Communist Party see no. 632.

611 О работе комсомола. Тезисы к XIV партсъезду, одобренные политбюро ЦК РКП(б). Москва, «Новая Москва,» 1925. 28 p.
NN NNC RZIA

612 О работе среди молодежи (1924). In: *Партия и воспитание смены* . . . See no. 620a; also no. 509.

613 О теории перманентной революции, by Bukharin and J. Stalin. **Артемьевск,** n. p., 1925. 46 p.

Bukharin's contribution includes: «Теория перманентной революции.» See no. 543.

614 Об «Уроках Октября» тов. Троцкого. Сборник статей и речей тт. Сталина, Бухарина и проч. Ростов-на-Дону, Буревестник, 1925. 231 p.

Contains Bukharin's article, Как не нужно писать историю Октября. По поводу книги тов. Троцкого «1917 г.» (1924). See no. 482; also no. 512.

615 Обоснование партийной программы . . . (1919). See no. 393.

616 Очередные задачи. Ленинград, «Кубуч,» 1925. 32 p.

617 Октябрь, by Bukharin, V. I. Lenin, and I. V. Stalin. Москва—Ленинград, Гос. изд., 1925. 176 p. *RZIA*

618 От капитализма к комунизму. Из «Азбуки коммунизма». (1919). See no. 194.

619 Памяти Ильича. In: *Правда,* no. 17, Jan. 21, 1925, pp. 1–2.

620 **Памяти М. В. Фрунзе.** In: *Правда,* no. 252, Nov. 3, 1925, p. 1.

620a **Партия и воспитание смены. Статьи и доклады.** (1924). See no. 516a; also no. 509.

621 **Переломный год нашего развития. Доклад тов. Н. И. Бухарина на 14-й Тульской губпартконференции.** Тула, Тулгубком, 1925. 38 p.

622 **Первая годовщина 1924. 21 января 1925. Ленин, о Ленине, о ленинизме,** by Bukharin *et al.* Москва, Московский рабочий, 1925. 327 p. *NN*

Contains Bukharin's Товарищ (1924). Ленинское воспитание молодежи (1924). Как работал Ленин (1924). Стоящие перед нами теоретические проблемы.

623 **Первая годовщина смерти Ленина,** by Bukharin *et al.* In: *Известия,* no. 18, Jan. 22, 1925, p. 4.

624 **Политическая экономия рантье . . .** (1919). See no. 239.

624a **Программа и устав РКП (большевиков). С докладами Н. И. Бухарина и В. И. Ленина на VIII съезде партии.** (1922). See no. 393.

625 **Пролетариат и вопросы художественной политики.** In: *Красная новь,* no. 4, 1925.

Also in:
Вопросы культуры при диктатуре пролетариата. Сборник, by Bukharin *et. al.* Москва—Ленинград, Гос. изд., 1925. 222 p. *NN*

626 **Пролетарская революция и культура.** (1923). See no. 443.

627 **Путь к социализму и рабоче-крестьянский союз.** Москва–Ленинград, Гос. изд., 1925. 106 p. *NNC CtY CSt-H*

Other editions:
Москва—Ленинград, Гос. изд., 1925. 106 p.
Москва—Ленинград, Гос. изд., 1927. 106 p. *NN MH WB*
Der Weg zum Sozialismus. Berlin, Verlag für Literatur und Politik, 1925. 125 p. *CSt-H*
Wien, Verlag für Literatur und Politik, 1925. 125 p. *NN NNC MH CtY CU DS UFU*
Wien, n. p., 1926. 126 p.
Le chemin du socialisme et le bloc ouvrier-paysan. Paris, Librairie de l'Humanité, 1925. 98 p. *NN CSt-H UL-H*

628 **«Рабселькоры — кусочек пролетарской демократии.»** In: *О рабкоре и селькоре . . .* See no. 698.

A speech delivered to a meeting of worker-correspondents of the Tatar Republic on May 28, 1925, but not published until 1926 in *О рабкоре и селькоре . . . .*

629 **Речь на XIV съезде РКП(б) 19 декабря 1925 года.** In: *Три речи . . .* See no. 722.

See no. 632 for a full account of Bukharin's remarks to the Fourteenth Congress of the Russian Communist Party.

630 **Речь на XIV Всероссийской конференции РКП(б) 29 апреля 1925 г.** In: *Три речи. . .* See no. 722.

See nos. 633 and 637 for a full record of Bukharin's remarks to the Fourteenth Conference of the Russian Communist Party.

631 **Речь на литературном совещании при ЦК ВКП(б) в феврале 1925.** In: *Вопросы культуры при диктатуре пролетариата. Сборник,* by Bukharin *et al.* Москва–Ленинград, Гос. изд., 1925. 222 p. *NN*

632 **[Remarks of Bukharin.]** In: *XIV съезд Всесоюзной Коммунистической партии (б). Стенографический отчет.* Москва—Ленинград, Гос. изд., 1926. 1029 p. *Available in various libraries.*

633 **[Remarks of Bukharin.]** In: *Четырнадцатая конференция Российской Коммунистической партии (большевиков). (Стенографический отчет).* Москва–Ленинград, Гос. изд., 1925. 335 p. *Available in various libraries.*

634 **[Remarks of Bukharin.]** In: (Fifth) *Расширенный Пленум Исполкома Коммунистического Интернационала. (Протоколы заседаний).* Москва—Ленинград, Гос. изд., 1925. 606 p. *NN NNC DLC*

635 **Report on Russian Communism to the Enlarged Executive Committee of the C. I.** In: *Inprecor,* V, no. 35, 1925.

See no. 634 for a complete record of Bukharin's remarks to the meeting of the Executive Committee of the Comintern; also nos. 596, 597, 602.

636 **[Resolution on the Tasks of the party],** by Bukharin *et al.* (1915). See no. 15.

637 **Speech of Comrade Bukharin in the Discussion on the NEP in the Village.** In: *Inprecor,* V, no. 46, 1925.

A translation of remarks to the Fourteenth Conference of the Russian Communist Party. See no. 633 for a full report of these remarks, as well as no. 630.

638 **The Stabilization of Capitalism, the Second International, and Ourselves.** (1924). In: *Inprecor,* V, no. 53, 1925.

A report to the Sixth Congress of the Komsomol. See no. 534 for a full report of Bukharin's remarks to the congress.

639 **Стоящие перед нами теоретические проблемы.** In: *Первая годовщина 1924 . . .* See no. 622.

640 **Судьбы русской интеллигенции.** In: *Печать и революция,* no. 3, 1925, pp. 1–10.

Also in:
Вопросы культуры при диктатуре пролетариата. Сборник, by Bukharin *et al.* Москва—Ленинград, Гос. изд., 1925. 222 p. *NN*
Судьбы современной интеллигенции. Доклад А. Луначарского и речи П. И. Сакулина, Н. И. Бухарина, Ю. В. Ключникова. Москва, Московский рабочий, 1925. 48 p. *NNC BDIC*

641 **Текущий момент и основы нашей политики. О решениях ЦК РКП(б) и XIV партконференции. Доклад на пленуме МК РКП(б).** Москва, Московский рабочий, 1925. 40 p. *NN CtY*

642 Текущий момент и политика партии. In: *Правда,* no. 137, June 19, 1925, p. 3.

Other editions:

Текущий момент и политика партии. Доклад тов. Н. И. Бухарина на VI Всесоюзной Конференции РЛКСМ. Ростов-на-Дону, n. p., 1925. 9 p.

643 Теория исторического материализма . . . (1921). See no. 377.

644 Теория перманентной революции. (1924). In: *К вопросу о троцкизме . . .* See no. 585.

Also in:

За ленинизм . . . See no. 654.

О теории перманентной революции . . . See no. 613.

See no. 543.

645 Товарищ (1924). In: *Первая годовщина 1924 . . .* See no. 622.

Also in:

О Ленине . . . See no. 607.

See main entry, no. 547.

646 Цезаризм под маской революции. По поводу книги Н. Устрялова «Под знаком революции.» Москва, Изд. газеты «Правда,» 1925. 45 p.
MH CSt-H DS

Other editions:

Москва, «Правда» и «Беднота,» 1925.

Нижний Новгород, n. p., 1925. 74 p.

Also in:

В защиту пролетарской диктатуры. Сборник. Москва—Ленинград, Гос. изд., 1928. 260 p.
NN DLC BrM DS BS RZIA

647 Über die Bauernfrage. Rede vor der Erweiterten Exekutive, April 1925. Hamburg, C. Hoym Nachfolger, 1925. 57 p.
NN MH DLC InU CSt-H

See no. 634 for a complete record of Bukharin's remarks to the Executive Committee of the Comintern.

Other editions:

La question paysanne, I. — Discours prononcé au plénum élargi du C. E. de l'Internationale Communiste le 2 avril 1925. II. — Thèse sur la question paysanne acceptée par l'executif élargi de l'I. C. Paris, Libraire de l'Humanité, 1925. 40 p.
CSt-H

N. p., n. p., 1926. 40 p.

648 Über die Theorie permanenten Revolution. In: *Um den Oktober* See no. 650; also no. 543.

649 Учительство и комсомол. Доклад на всесоюзном съезде учителей. In: *Правда,* no. 28, Feb. 4, 1925, p. 5.

Other editions:

Учительство и комсомол. Доклад на всесоюзном съезде учителей. Москва, Новая Москва, 1925. 22 p. *CSt-H RZIA*
Москва, n. p., 1925.

Les instituteurs et la jeunesse communiste; discours prononcé au congrès des instituteurs de l'U.R.S.S., janvier 1925. Paris, l'Internationale des Travailleurs de l'Enseignement, 1925. 16 p. *NN NNC CSt-H UL-H*

650 Um den Oktober, by Bukharin *et al.* Hamburg, n. p., 1925. *CSt-H UFU*

Bukharin's contribution includes: Über die Theorie der permanenten Revolution. See no. 543.

651 The Visit of the German Workers' Delegation to the Soviet Union. In: *Inprecor,* V. no. 59, 1925. See nos. 602 and 663.

652 Вопросы культуры при диктатуре пролетариата. Сборник, by Bukharin *et al.* Москва–Ленинград, Гос. изд., 1925. 222 p. *NN*

Bukharin's contribution includes: О политике партии в художественной литературе (1924) — Пролетариат и вопросы художественной политики — Речь на литературном совещании при ЦК ВКП(б) в феврале 1925. Судьбы русской интеллигенции.

653 Das Wirtschaftliche Wachstum und das Problem des Arbeiter- und Bauernblocks (1924). See no. 484.

654 За ленинизм. Сборник статей, by Bukharin *et al.* Москва—Ленинград, Гос. изд., 1925. 488 p. *NN*

Bukharin's contribution includes: Новое откровение о советской экономике, или как можно погубить рабоче-крестьянский блок ... (1924) — Как не нужно писать историю Октября (1924) — Теория перманентной революции (1924). See main entries for each of these titles under the years of their original writing or publication as indicated.

655 **Значение аграрно-крестьянской проблемы.** In: *Большевик,* no. 3/4, Feb. 25, 1925, pp. 3–17.

1926

656 **3-е Всесоюзное совещание рабселькоров. Ответная речь Н. И. Бухарина.** In: *Правда,* no. 119, May 26, 1926, p. 3. See nos. 657 and 697.

657 **3-е Всесоюзное совещание рабселькоров. Речь тов. Н. И. Бухарина.** In: *Правда,* no. 118, May 25, 1926, p. 3. See nos. 656 and 697.

658 **VII Meeting of the Enlarged ECCI.** In: *Inprecor,* VI, nos. 83, 85, 88, 1926; VII, no. 2, 1927.

See no. 717 for a full report of Bukharin's remarks to the session; also no. 661.

659 **The XIV Party Congress of the CP of Russia. Discussion of the Political Report** (1925). In: *Inprecor,* VI, no. 5, 1926.

See no. 632 for a full report of Bukharin's remarks to the Fourteenth Congress of the Russian Communist Party; also nos. 680 and 722.

660 **The XV Party Conference of the CP of USSR. Questions of International Politics.** In: *Inprecor,* VI, nos. 72, 73, 1925.

See no. 716 for a full record of Bukharin's remarks to the Conference; also no. 671.

661 **«Апелляция» оппозиции. Речь на VII расширенном пленуме исполнительного комитета Коммунистического Интернационала 8 декабря 1926 г.**

This item is a speech delivered by Bukharin to the Seventh Enlarged Plenum of the Executive Committee of the Comintern in December 1926, but not published until 1927. See no. 733. For a complete record of Bukharin's remarks to the session, see no. 717; also no. 658.

662 **Борьба за кадры. Речи и статьи.** Москва–Ленинград, «Молодая гвардия,» 1926. 350 p. *DS RZIA*

663 **Bucharins Antwort an sozialdemokratische Arbeiter.** Berlin, Vereinigung Internationaler Verlagsanstalten, 1926. 31 p. See nos. 602 and 651.
NNC BDIC

664 **Capitalist Stabilization and Proletarian Revolution; Report to the VII Enlarged Plenum of the E. C. of the Comintern on Point I on the Agenda: "The World Situation and the Tasks of the Comintern."** Moscow, The Executive Committee of the Comintern, 1926. 108 p.
NN CSt-H

A reprint of Bukharin's speech to the Seventh Plenum of the Executive Committee of the Comintern, delivered in 1926 and published in that year in English and in German, and in Russian in 1927. For a complete record of Bukharin's remarks to the session, see no. 717.

Other editions:

Die kapitalistische Stabilisierung und die proletarische Revolution; Bericht an das VII erweiterte Plenum des Exekutivkomitees der Komintern zum I. Punkt der Tagesordnung: "Die Weltlage und die Aufgaben der Kommunistischen Internationale." Moskau, EKKI, 1926. 128 p. *NN BS*

Капиталистическая стабилизация и пролетарская революция. Доклад и заключительное слово по первому пункту порядка дня: «О международном положении и задачах Коминтерна» на VII Расширенном пленуме Исполнительного Комитета Коммунистического Интернационала с приложением тезисов, принятых пленумом. Москва—Ленинград, Гос. изд., 1927. 347 p. *NN NNC MH DLC CtY NjP RZIA DS*

Капиталистическая стабилизация и пролетарская революция. Доклад VII Расширенному пленуму Исполнительного Комитета Коммунистического Интернационала по первому пункту порядка дня: «Мировое положение и задачи Коминтерна.» Москва—Ленинград, Гос. изд., 1927. 213 p.
DLC

Also in:

Die kapitalistische Stabilisierung und die proletarische Revolution, sowie 3 Diskussionbeiträge auf der 7. Tagung des erweiterten EKKI. In: *Internationale Presse-Korrespondenz,* VI, no, 147, 1926, pp. 2575-2610; no. 148, pp. 2611-2625; no. 152, pp. 2679-2742; no. 155, pp. 2767-2810; no. 156, pp. 2811-2834; no. 158, pp. 2855-2898; no. 160, pp. 2913-2948; VII, no. 2, 1927, pp. 18-52; no. 4, pp. 65-95; no. 8, pp. 149-168; no. 9, pp. 169-184; no. 16, pp. 313-346.

665 **Что решил XIV партсъезд?** In: *Ставрополье,* no. 1, 1926, pp. 5–53.

666 **Диктатура пролетариата и рабкоровские организации.** (1924). In: *О рабкоре и селькоре . . .* See no. 698; also no. 467.

667 **Discussion on Comrade Stalin's Report.** In: *Inprecor,* VI, no. 78, 1926.

This item is a reprint of Bukharin's remarks at the Fifteenth Conference of the Communist Party of the Soviet Union; see no. 716 for a complete record of his remarks to the Conference.

668 **Доклад на XXIII чрезвычайной Ленинградской губернской конференции ВКП(б).** Москва–Ленинград, Гос. изд., 1926. 59 p. See no. 677. *CSt-H*

Other editions:
Москва—Ленинград, Гос. изд., 1926. 54 p. *NNC*
Москва—Ленинград, n. p., 1926. 48 p.

669 **Два слова о некоторых особенностях рабкоровской работы.** (1924). In: *О рабкоре и селькоре* . . . See no. 698; also no. 470.

670 **Феликс Дзержинский умер.** In: *Правда,* no. 165, July 21, 1926, p. 1.

Also in:
Felix Dzershinsky is Dead. In: *Inprecor,* VI, no. 54, 1926.

671 **Die Frage der internationalen Politik. Referat auf der 15. Unionskonferenz der KPSR.** In: *Internationale Presse-Korrespondenz,* VI, no. 130, pp. 2235–2248.

See no. 716 for a complete account of Bukharin's remarks to the Fifteenth Conference of the Russian Communist Party; also no. 660.

672 **Historical Materialism . . .** (1921). See no. 377.

673 **Der Imperialismus und die Akkumulation des Kapitals.** (1924). See no. 477.

674 **Империализм и накопление капитала . . .** (1924). See no. 477.

675 **Итоги перевыборов советов.** In: *Агитатор,* no. 17, 1926, pp. 9–15.

A report by Bukharin to the Leningrad section of the Russian Communist Party, delivered on July 28, 1926.

676 **К итогам XIV съезда ВКП(б).** In: *Правда,* no. 8, Jan. 10, 1926, pp. 5–6; no. 9, Jan. 12, 1926, pp. 3–4.

Other editions:

К итогам XIV съезда РКП(б). Доклад на собрании активных работников Московской организации 5-го января 1926 г. Москва—Ленинград, Московский рабочий, 1926. 63 p. *RZIA*
Москва—Ленинград, n. p., 1926. 50 p.
Ленинград, n. p., 1926. 62 p.

Итоги XIV съезда ВКП(б). Нижний Новгород, Нижне-Новгородская коммуна, 1926. 95 p.

Also in:

К итогам XIV съезда ВКП(б). In: *Авангард,* no. 1/2, 1926, pp. 3—49.
К итогам XIV съезда ВКП(б). In: *За Работой,* no. 1/2, 1926, pp. 1—24.

677 **К итогам дискуссии. Доклады на XXIII чрезвычайной Ленинградской губернской, Выборгской и Московско-Нарвской районных конференциях ВКП(б).** Ленинград, n. p., 1926. 114 p. See no. 668.

678 **К критике экономической платформы оппозиции. Уроки октября 1923 г.** (1924–1925). In: *Критика экономической платформы оппозиции.* See no. 687; also no. 582.

679 **К вопросу о международной связи.** (1924). In: *О рабкоре и селькоре . . .* See no. 698; also no. 479.

680 **К вопросу о наших разногласиях. Речь на XIV съезде РКП(б).** (1925). Ленинград, n. p., 1926. 24 p.

See no. 632 for a complete record of Bukharin's remarks to the Fourteenth Congress of the Russian Communist Party; also no. 722.

681 **К вопросу о закономерностях переходного периода.** In: *Правда,* no. 148, July 1, 1926, p. 3; no. 150, July 3, 1926, pp. 2–3; no. 154, July 7, 1926, pp. 2–3.

Other editions:

К вопросу о закономерностях переходного периода. Критические замечания на книгу Е. Преображенского «Новая экономика.» Москва—Ленинград, «Мосполиграф,» 1928. 92 p. *WB*

682 **К вопросу об изучении ленинизма.** In: *Правда,* no. 17, Jan. 21, 1926, p. 2.

683 **К вопросу об организации рабкоров и селькоров.** (1924). In: *О рабкоре и селькоре . . .* See no. 698; also no. 481.

684 **Какой должна быть молодеж? Наши основные задачи и молодежь.** In: *Молодая гвардия,* no. 2, Feb. 1926, pp. 73–92.

This item is a reprint of a speech delivered by Bukharin to the tenth Moscow provincial conference of the Komsomol.

685 **Капиталистическая стабилизация и пролетарская революция . . .**

The title of a reprint of Bukharin's speech to the Seventh Enlarged Plenum of the Executive Committee of the Comintern, delivered in 1926 but not published in Russian until 1927 (see no. 664; for a complete record of Bukharin's remarks to the meeting, see no. 717).

686 **Karl Kautsky und Sowjetrussland. Eine Antwort.** (1925). See no. 598.

687 **Крититка экономической платформы оппозиции.** Ленинград, «Прибой,» 1926. 92 p. *NN MH CSt-H CtY ICU DS*

Contents. — К критике экономической платформы оппозиции . . . (1924—1925). — Новое откровение о советской экономике, или как можно погубить рабоче-крестьянский блок (1924).
See main entries for each of the two essays, nos. 582 and 502a, respectively.

Other editions:
Ленинград, «Прибой,» 1926, 92 p.

688 **Ленин как тип мыслителя.** In: *Правда,* no. 93, Apr. 23, 1926, p. 2.

689 **Мировое хозяйство и империализм . . .** (1917). See no. 82.

690 **На чем нужно обучаться равкорам.** (1924). In: *О рабкоре и селькоре . . .* See no. 698; see also no. 500.

691 **На подступах к Октябрю. Статьи и речи май—декабрь 1917 г.** Москва—Ленинград, Гос. изд., 1926. 188 p. *NN CSt-H CtY OCl BDIC*

This collection of articles, which for the most part appeared originally in *Социал-демократ* and *Спартак* during 1917, is especially valuable inasmuch as the originals are not accessible in the West.

Contents. — 1. Предисловие. — 2. Петроградский Совет Р. и С. Д. и Армия. — 3. Они недовольны. — 4. Военная дороговизна. — 5. Три направления в старой социал-демократии. — 6. До каких пор ждать? — 7. Либералы и городские служащие. — 8. Российская революция и ее судьбы. — 9. Клеветники. — 10. Государственный контроль над производством и русская буржуазия. — 11. Буржуазные патриоты и «Заем свободы.» — 12. Организованное творчество. — 13. Русское наступление и цели союзников. — 14. Где контр-революция? — 15. Еще одно «освобождение.» — 16. Нота Временного правительства. — 17. Слова и дела. — 18. Вперед. — 19. По поводу съезда Советов рабочих и солдатских депутатов. — 20. Министерские мероприятия. — 21. Торжественное заявление. — 22. По поводу наступления. — 23. О наступлении на фронте. — 24. О наступлении. — 25. Экономический развал и война. — 26. Натиск капиталистов. — 27. Парижсякая коммуна и революционная Россия. — 28. Еще раз о товарише Ленине. — 29. Поражение или победа? — 30. «Сотрудничество всех классов.» — 31. Кризис власти. — 32. Манифест VI съезда РСДРП(б). — 33. Иезуитский штаб контрреволюции. — 34. Планы генералов. — 35. Экономическая политика промышлеников, Московское совещание и демократия. — 36. «Общенациональные задачи» и гражданская война. — 37. К вопросу о земельных захватах. — 38. Международная революция. — 39. Чудовищное предательство. — 40. Восстановление самодержавия? — 41. Мелкие заметки. — 42. Советы прежде и теперь. — 43. Кадетский съезд. — 44. Развернутый фронт. — 45. 19-е октября в Московских Советах. — 46. Громят Советы. — 47. Экономика и политика. — 48. К социализму. — 49. Крах империалистического правительства. — 50. Из-за чего борьба? — 51. Новая революция и международный капитал. — 52. Чего хотят большевики? — 53. Маски долой. — 54. Каледин и Авксентьев. — 55. Герой лжи и подлога. — 56. Манифест Военно-революционного комитета. — 57. Черносотенные «социалисты.» — 58. О Московских событиях. — 59. Речь на первом заседании Учредительного собрания.

692 **На пороге десятого года.** In: *Правда,* no. 258, Nov. 7, 1926, p. 2.

693 **Новая программа Австрийской социал-демократии.** In: *Правда,* no. 214, Sept. 17, 1926, pp. 2–3.

Also in:

Новая программа Австрийской социал-демократии. In: *Коммунистический Интернационал,* no. 1 (59), Sept. 1926, pp. 11—23.

Das neue Programm der österreichischen Sozialdemokratie. In: *Die Kommunistische Internationale,* VII, no. 1 (10), 1926, pp. 8—17.

694 **Новое откровение о советской экономике, или как можно погубить рабоче-крестьянский блок . . .** (1924). In: *Критика экономической платформы оппозиции.* See no. 687; also no. 502a.

695 О характере нашей революции и о возможности победоносного социалистического строительства в СССР. In: *Большевик,* no. 19/20, Oct. 1926, pp. 28–59.

Other editions:

О характере нашей революции и о возможности победоносного социалистического строительства в СССР. Ленинград, «Прибой,» 1926. 79 p. *NN DLC*

Fragen des sozialistischen Aufbaues. Hamburg, C. Hoym Nachfolger, 1926. 51 p. Berlin, C. Hoym Nachfolger, 1926. 50 p. *NN MH CSt-H*

Les problèmes de l'édification socialiste. Caractère de la révolution d'Octobre et possibilités de victoire de l'édification socialiste en U.R.S.S. Paris, Malakoff, Impr. Coopérative "la Typo-Litho," 1926. 36 p. *BiN UL-H CSt-H*

Building Up Socialism. London, Communist Party of Great Britain, 1926. 66 p. *NNC MH NjP CU CLU InU WaU OFU-W CSt-H*

Also in:

В защиту пролетарской диктатуры. Сборник. Москва—Ленинград, Гос. изд., 1928. 260 p. *NN DLC BrM DS BS RZIA*

696 О международном положении. Доклад на собрании активных работников Ленинградской организации ВКП(б) 11 июня 1926 года. Ленинград, «Прибой,» 1926. 47 p. *NNC DLC*

Other editions:

Ленинград, «Прибой,» 1926. 47 p.

697 О партийном руководстве рабселькорами. In: *Правда,* no. 121, May 28, 1926, pp. 3–4. See nos. 656 and 657.

Other editions:

Партаия и руководство рабселькорами. Доклад и заключительное слово на 3-м всесоюзном совещании рабселькоров при «Правде» и «Рабоче-крестъянском корреспонденте». Москва, «Правда» и «Беднота», 1926. 40 p.

698 О рабкоре и селькоре. Статьи и речи. Москва, «Правда» и «Беднота,» 1926. 77 p. *NNC MH BiN RZIA DS*

The preface of this item states that it is a second, revised and enlarged edition of a collection first published in 1924 under the title, *О рабкоре.* There is no known available copy of this earlier edition, and comparisons between the two cannot be made. By inference from the preface to the 1926 edition, most, but not all, of the articles and speeches antedating 1925 and printed in the 1926 edition were originally included in the 1924 edition, but this cannot be verified. All titles within the item are cross-referenced here, both under 1926 and the year of origin.

Contents. — Заветы Ленина и рабкоры (1924). — Диктатура пролетариата и рабкоровские организации (1924). — Два слова о некоторых особенностях рабкоровской работы (1924). — На чем нужно обучаться рабкорам (1924). — Вопросы первого Всесоюзного совещания рабкоров (1923). — К вопросу о международной связи (1924). — Против рабкоровского профсоюза (1924). — О селькорах и нашей политике в деревне (1924). — Об убийстве селькора Малиновского (1924). К вопросу об организации рабкоров и селькоров (1924). «Рабселькоры — кусочек пролетарской демократии» (1925).

699 О работе комсомола. Доклад на XIV съезде РКП(б). Ленинград, n. p., 1926. 30 p. *NN NNC RZIA*

This report to the Fourteenth Congress of the Russian Communist Party was delivered in December 1925 and published separately in 1926. See no. 632 for a full account of Bukharin's remarks to the Congress.

Other editions:
Ленинград, n. p., 1926. 30 p.

О работе РЛКСМ. Доклад на XIV съезде ВКП(б). Москва-Ленинград, n. p., 1926. 60 p.
Москва—Ленинград, n. p., 1926. 60 p.

О работе комсомола. Доклад и заключительное слово на XIV съезде ВКП(б). С приложением резолюции о работе комсомола. Москва—Ленинград, n. p., 1926. 48 p.

700 О селькорах и нашей политике в деревне. (1924). In: *О рабкоре и селькоре . . .* See no. 698; also no. 510.

701 Об экономической платформе оппозиции. Сборник статей, by Bukharin *et al.* Москва, Гос. изд., 1926. 446 p. *MH*

702 Об убийстве селькора Малиновского. (1924). In: *О рабкоре и селькоре . . .* See no. 698; also no. 511.

703 Очередные надежды и очередные иллюзии. In: *Правда,* no. 2, Jan. 3, 1926, p. 1.

704 Памяти тов. Ф. Е. Дзержинского. Речь тов. Н. И. Бухарина. In: *Правда,* no. 168, July 24, 1926, p. 5.

Other editions:
Пролетарский якобинец. Памяти Ф. Е. Дзержинского. Москва—Ленинград, «Московский рабочий,» 1926. 14 p.

705 Партия и оппозиционный блок. In: *Правда,* no. 176, Aug. 3, 1926, p. 3.

This item is a report of a speech delivered by Bukharin on July 28, 1926, to a meeting of Party activists of the Leningrad organization.

Other editions:

Партия и оппозиционный блок. Ленинград, «Прибой,» 1926. 125 p. *NN DLC RZIA WB BS*

Ленинград, n. p., 1926. 125 p.

Москва—Ленинград, Гос. изд., 1926. 65 p. *DLC CU*

Ленинград, «Прибой,» 1926. 132 p. *DLC InU CSt-H*

Партия и опозиционный блок. С приложением резолюции и постановлений объединенного пленума ЦК и ЦКК ВКП(б) 14—23 июля 1926 г. и постановления ЦКК ВКП(б) по делу Т. Беленького, Чернышева и др., by Bukharin and A. Rykov. Москва—Ленинград, Гос. изд., 1926 144 p. *NNC CtY ICU RZIA*

Москва—Ленинград, Гос. изд., 1926. 144 p.

Also in:

The Party and the Opposition Bloc. In: *Inprecor,* VI, nos. 57, 58, 1926.

The Party and the Opposition Bloc. In: *The Communist Review,* Sept. 5, 1926, pp. 208-218; Oct. 6, pp. 267-281; Nov. 7, pp. 326-336.

706 Die politische Ökonomie des Rentners . . . (1919). See no. 239.

707 Против рабкоровского профсоюза. (1924). In: *О рабкоре и селькоре . . .* See no. 698; also no. 527.

708 La question paysanne . . . (1925). See no. 647.

709 «Рабселькоры — кусочек пролетарской демократии». (1925). In: *О рабкоре и селькоре . . .* See no. 698; also no. 628.

710 Речь на XIV Московской губпартконференции 6 декабря 1925 г. (1925). In: *Три речи . . .* See no. 722; also no. 564.

711 Речь на XIV съезде РКП(б) 19 декабря 1925 года. (1925). In: *Три речи . . .* See no. 722.

See no. 632 for a complete record of Bukharin's remarks to the Fourteenth Congress of the Russian Communist Party.

712 Речь на XIV Всероссийской конференции РКП(б) 29 апреля 1925 г. (1925). In: *Три речи . . .* See no. 722.

See no. 633 for a complete record of Bukharin's remarks to the Fourteenth Conference of the Russian Communist Party.

713 Речь на первом заседании Учредительного собрания. (1918). In: *На подступах к Октябрю . . .* See no. 691; also see no. 168.

714 Речь тов. Н. И. Бухарина в Германской комиссии VI пленума Коммунистического Интернационала. In: *Коммунистический Интернационал,* no. 3 (52), Mar. 1926, pp. 92–103.

See no. 727.

715 [Remarks of Bukharin.] In: *VII съезд Всесоюзного Ленинского Коммунистического Союза Молодежи. Стенографический отчет.* Москва–Ленинград, Молодая гвардия, 1926. 516 p. *NN*

716 [Remarks of Bukharin.] In: *XV конференция Всесоюзной Коммунистической партии (б). Стенографический отчет.* Москва–Ленинград, Гос. изд., 1927. 845 p. *Available in various libraries.*

717 [Remarks of Bukharin.] In: *Пути мировой революции. Седьмой расширенный пленум Исполнительного Комитета Коммунистического Интернационала. Стенографический отчет.* Москва–Ленинград, Гос. изд., 1927. 2 vols. *NN NNC*

718 [Remarks of Bukharin.] In: *Седьмой съезд профессиональных союзов СССР. Пленумы и секции. Полный стенографический отчет.* Москва, Всесоюзный центральный совет профсоюзов, 1927. 1028 p. *NN*

719 [Remarks of Bukharin.] In: *Шестой расширенный пленум исполкома Коминтерна. Стенографический отчет.* Москва–Ленинград Гос., изд., 1927. 707 p. *NNC*

720 **«Рычи Китай» в театре Мейерхолда.** In: *Правда,* no. 26, Feb. 2, 1926, p. 3.

721 **Sosialidemokraatit ja Neuvostoliitto.** Kuopiossa, n. p., 1926. 176 p. *MH*

Also in:
The Russian Revolution and Social Democracy. In: *Inprecor,* VII, no. 68, 1927.

722 **Три речи (К вопросу о наших разногласиях).** Москва–Ленинград, Гос. изд., 1926. 69 p. *NN CU RZIA WB*

Contents. — Речь на XIV Московской губпартконференции 6 декабря 1925 г. (see main entry, no. 564). — Речь на XIV съезде РКП(б) 19 декабря 1925 года. — Речь на XIV Всероссийской конференции РКП(б) 29 апреля 1925 г.

For complete records of Bukharin's remarks to the Fourteenth Congress and the Fourteenth Conference of the Russian Communist Party, see nos. 632 and 633, respectively.

722a **Вопрос о нэпе.** In: *Спутник большевика,* no. 1 (10), 1926(?).

723 **Вопросы международной революционной борьбы.** In: *Правда,* no. 144, June 26, 1926, p. 3.

Also in:
Questions of the International Revolutionary Struggle. In: *Inprecor,* VI, nos. 51, 52, 1926.

724 **Вопросы первого всесоюзного совещания рабкоров.** (1923). In: *О рабкоре и селькоре . . .* See no. 698; also no. 454.

725 **Der Weg zum Sozialismus.** (1925). See no. 627.

726 **Заветы Ленина и рабкоры.** (1924). In: *О рабкоре и селькоре . . .* See no. 698; also no. 560.

727 **Zur deutschen Frage.** In: *Die Kommunistische Internationale,* VII, no. 5, 1926, pp. 270–283.

See no. 714.

1927

728 VII Enlarged Meeting of the ECCI. (1926). See no. 658.

729 XV Московская губернская партийная конференция. Речь тов. Бухарина. In: *Правда,* no. 7, Jan. 9, 1927, p. 3. See nos. 730 and 762.

730 XV Московская губпартконференция. Заключительное слово тов. Н. И. Бухарина. In: *Правда,* no. 12, Jan. 15, 1927, p. 3. See nos. 729 and 762.

731 XVI Московская губернская партийная конференция. Доклад тов. Н. И. Бухарина. In: *Правда,* no. 268, Nov. 23, 1927, pp. 3–4; no. 269, Nov. 24, 1927, p. 4; no. 271, Nov. 26, 1927, p. 2.

Other editions:
За ленинизм, by N. Bukharin and I. Stalin. N. p., n. p., 1927.
A reprint of the speeches delivered by Bukharin and Stalin to the Sixteenth Conference of the Moscow section of the Party. Precise contents and location of this item are unknown.
Очередные задачи партии. Доклад на XVI Московской губернской парт-конференции 20 ноября 1927 г. Москва—Ленинград, Гос. изд., 1928. 125 p. *DS BS RZIA*

Also in:
The Menshevik Character of the Ideology and Tactics of the Opposition. In *Inprecor,* VII, no. 69, 1927.
Der menschewistische Charakter der Ideologie und der Taktik der Opposition. In *Internationale Presse-Korrespondenz,* VII, no. 117, 1927, pp. 2617-2620.

732 The A B C of Communism . . . (1919). See no. 194.

733 «Апелляция» оппозиции. Речь на VII расширенном пленуме Исполнительного Комитета Коммунистического Интернационала 8 декабря 1926. г. Москва—Ленинград, Гос. изд., 1927. 46 p. *RZIA*

See no. 717 for a complete record of Bukharin's remarks to the seventh plenum of the Executive Committee of the Comintern, held in 1926.

734 **Le communisme et la question nationale et coloniale, Par Lénine, Staline et Boukharine.** Paris, Impr. Centrale, 1927 64 p. *BiN*

Other editions:
Paris, Bureau d'Éditions de Diffusion et de Publicité, 1928.
Paris, Bureau d'Éditions de Diffusion et de Publicité, 193-? 60 p. *IU*

735 **The Developments in the Chinese Revolution.** In: *The Communist International,* IV, no. 11, 1927.

736 **Доклад. XXIV Ленинградская губпартконференция.** In: *Правда,* no. 26, Feb. 2, 1927, pp. 3–4.

Also in:
We must Be Prepared. In: *Inprecor,* VII, no. 12, 1927.
The International Situation. In: *Inprecor,* VII, no. 14, 1927.
Zur internationalen Lage. In: *Internationale Presse-Korrespondenz,* VII, no. 17, 1927, pp. 349—352.

737 **The Economic Theory of the Leisure Class.** (1919). See no. 239.

738 **Экономические перспективы в деревне.** In: *Правда,* no. 254, Nov. 5, 1927, pp. 4–5.

Also in:
Für die Leninsche Linie in den Fragen der Politik auf dem Dorfe; die ökonomischen Perspektiven im Dorfe. In: *Internationale Presse-Korrespondenz,* VII, no. 118, 1927, pp. 2679—2682.
For the Leninist Line in the Question of Our Policy in the Village. In *Inprecor,* VII, no. 70, 1927.

739 **Героическая песнь (Чекист Феликс Дзержинский).** In: *Правда,* no. 290, Dec. 18, 1927, p. 1.

740 **Годовщина славной и трагической смерти.** In: *Правда,* no. 162, July 20, 1927, p. 1.

This article commemorated the death of Felix Dzerzhinsky.

741 **The Grouping of the Classes Before March.** (1917). See no. 68.

742 Der Imperialismus und die Akkumulation des Kapitals. (1924). See no. 477.

743 Империализм и накопление капитала... (1924). See no. 477.

744 [Introduction to] A. Aikhenval'd, Советская экономика... See no. 845.

The introduction to this book, which was not published until 1929, was written by Bukharin in 1927.

745 Итоги пленума ИККИ. In: *Правда,* no. 135, June 18, 1927, p. 3.

Other editions:

Итоги пленума ИККИ. Доклад тов. Н. И. Бухарина на пленуме московского комитета ВКП(б) 4 июня. Москва, «Правда» и «Беднота,» 1927. 54 p. *NN*

О китайской революции. Статья Н. Бухарина и постановление ИККИ. Иркутск, АПО Иркутского комитета РКП(б), 1927. 29 p.
This item is a reprint of part of Bukharin's report to the meeting of the Moscow Committee of the Russian Communist Party. It was also printed in *Вопросы китайской революции* (see no. 787).

Also in:

Die Ergebnisse des Plenums des EKKI. Bericht, erstellt auf dem Plenum des Moskauer Komitees der KPSU am 4 Juni 1927. In: *Internationale Presse-Korrespondenz,* VII, no. 65, 1927, pp. 1361—1373.

The Results of the Plenary Session of the ECCI. In: *Inprecor,* VII, nos. 37, 39, 1927.

746 The July Victory of the Counter-Revolution. (1918).

A reprint of part of *От диктатуры империализма к диктатуре пролетариата...* See no. 160.

747 К десятилетию Октябрьской революции. In: *Правда,* no. 255, Nov. 6–7, 1927, p. 3.

This item should not be confused with the following entry, which has the same title.

748 К десятилетию Октябрьской революции. In: *Правда,* no. 237, Oct. 16, 1927, pp. 5–6; no. 238, Oct. 18, 1927, p. 5.

A speech to the Seventh Moscow Provincial Congress of Trade Unions.

Other editions:

К десятилетию Октябрьской революции. Доклад на VII Московском губернском съезде профсоюзов 12 октября 1927 года. Москва, Гос. изд., 1927. 78 p. *NN MH CSt-H BDIC BM-P*
Нижний Новгород, n. p., 1927. 90 p.

Also in:

10 Jahre Sowjetmacht, 10 Jahre siegreiche proletarische Revolution. Bericht auf dem 7. Moskauer Gouvernements-Gewerkschaftskongress. In: *Internationale Presse-Korres-*

pondenz, VII, no. 104, 1927, pp. 2249—2253; no. 105, pp. 2277—2280, 2333—2336; no. 108, pp. 2357—2359.

Ten Years of Victorious Proletarian Revolution. In: *Inprecor,* VII, nos. 61, 63, 1927.

749 К десятой годовщине Февральской революции. Речь на торжественном собрании в Большом театре 12 марта 1927 года. Москва, Гос. изд., 1927. 31 p. *NN*

Also in:

Zum 10. Jahrestag der Februarrevolution. In: *Internationale Presse-Korrespondenz,* VII, no. 32, 1927, pp. 685-688; no. 33, pp. 718-719; no. 34, pp. 741-743.

The Tenth Anniversary of the February Revolution. In: *Inprecor,* VII, nos. 21, 22, 1927.

750 К постановке проблем теории исторического материализма (беглые заметки). (1923). In: *La théorie matérialisme historique ... suivie d'une note sur la position du problème du matérialisme historique.* See no. 377; also see no. 420.

751 Капиталическая стабилизация и пролетарская революция . . . (1926). See no. 664.

752 Die kapitalistische Stabilisierung und die proletarische Revolution . . . (1926). See no. 664.

753 The Kornilov Putsch and the Resistance of the Working Class. (1918).

A reprint of part of *От диктатуры империализма к диктатуре пролетариата ...* See no. 160.

754 Культурные задачи и борьба с бюрократизмом. In: *Революция и культура,* no. 2, Dec. 5, 1927, pp. 5—12.

755 Ленинизм и строительный период пролетарской революции. In: *Правда,* no. 17, Jan. 21, 1927, p. 2.

Also in:

Ленинизм и строительный период пролетарской революции. In: *Под знаменем коммунизма,* I, no. 1, 1927, pp. 7—15.

756 Лозунг советов в Венском восстании. Из речи тов. Н. И. Бухарина в политсекретариате ИККИ. In: *Коммунистический Интернационал,* no. 43 (117), Oct. 1927, pp. 11–13.

757 Международное положение и задачи Коммунистического Интернационала. In: *Правда,* no. 285, Dec. 13, 1927, pp. 1–4; no. 286, Dec. 14, 1927, pp. 1–2.

A speech delivered by Bukharin to the Fifteenth Congress of the Russian Communist Party. See no. 777 for a full record of his remarks to the congress.

Other editions:

Отчет делегации ВКП(б) в ИККИ XV съезду ВКП(б). Международное положение и задачи Коммунистического Интернационала. Доклад и заключительное слово 9—12 декабря 1927 г. Москва, Гос., изд., 1928. 204 p. *CSt-H*

Отчет делегации ВКП(б) в ИККИ XV съезду ВКП(б). Доклад и заключительное слово. С приложением резолюции съезда. N. p., n. p., 19-? 124 p.

Die internationale Lage und die Aufgaben der Kommunistischen Internationale. Bericht der Delegation der KPSU(B) beim EKKI an den 15. Parteitag. Referat des Genossen N. Bucharin. Hamburg—Berlin, C. Hoym Nachfolger, 1928. 69 p. *NN MH CU IU*

La Situation internationale et les tâches de l'I. C. Rapport au XVeme Congrès du P. C. l'U.R.S.S. Paris, Bureau d'Éditions, 1928. 104 p. *NN MH*

Also in:

Die internationale Lage und die Aufgaben der Kommunistischen Internationale. Referat und Schlusswort auf dem 15. Parteitag. In: *Internationale Presse-Korrespondenz,* VII, no. 123, 1927, pp. 2913—2921.

[Report of Bukharin, Международное положение и задачи Коммунистического Интернационала]. In: *Report of the Fifteenth Congress of the Communist Party of the Soviet Union.* London, n. p., 1928. pp. 196—280.

The International Position and the Tasks of the Communist International. In: *Inprecor,* VII, no. 73, 1927; VIII, no. 1, 1928.

758 Мировое хозяйство и империализм... (1917). See no. 82.

759 На крутом перевале китайской революции. In: *Правда,* no. 154, July 10, 1927, pp. 2–3.

Other editions:

На крутом перевале китайской революции. Нижний Новгород, «Нижег. Коммуна», 1927. 50 p.

Also in:

An einem jähen Wendpunkte der chinesischen Revolution. In: *Internationale Presse-Korrespondenz,* VII, no. 70, 1927, pp. 1485—1488; no. 71, pp. 1511—1513.

An Abrupt Turn in the Chinese Revolution. In: *Inprecor,* VII, nos. 41, 42, 1927.

760 Наука и СССР. In: *Большевик,* no. 17, 1927.

Other editions:
Наука и СССР. Ленинград, Работник просвещения, 1928. 15 p. *MH DLC*
Ленинград, Тип. «Коминтерн,» 1928. 15 p. *CSt-H*
Also in:
Наука и техника за десять лет, by Bukharin *et al.* Москва, Работник просвещения, 1927—1928. 3 vols.
Science and the Soviet Union. In: *Inprecor,* VII, nos. 60, 61, 1927.

761 Die neuesten Erscheinungen der Stabilisierung des Kapitalismus. Aus der Rede des Genossen Bucharin im letzten Plenum des ZK der KPSU. In: *Die Kommunistische Internationale,* VIII, no. 37, 1927, pp. 1784–1796.

761a О китайской революции. Статья Н. И. Бухарина и постановление ИККИ. Иркутск, АПО Иркутского комитета РКП(б), 1927. 29 p. See no. 745.

Also in:
Вопросы китайской революции. Москва—Ленинград, Гос. изд., 1927. 240 p. *NN CSt-H*

762 О международном и внутреннем положении СССР. Доклад тов. Н. И. Бухарина на XV Московской губпартконференции. In: *Правда,* no. 10, Jan. 13, 1927, pp. 2–4. See nos. 729 and 730.

Other editions:
О международном и внутреннем положении СССР. Доклад, заключительное слово на XV Московской губпартконференции и резолюция по докладу. Москва. «Правда» и «Беднота,» 1927. 107 p. *MH DLC RZIA*

Москва, n. p., 1927. 107 p.
Москва, Московский рабочий, 1927. 75 p.
О международном и внутреннем положении СССР. Доклад на XV Московской губпартконференции. Нижний Новгород, n. p., 1927. 75 p. *DS*
Международное и внутреннее положение СССР. Доклад на XV Московской губпартконференции. Москва, Московский рабочий, 1927. 46 p. *MH CtY DLC*
Die internationale und innere Lage der USSR. Referat gehalten auf der 15. Moskauer Gouvernements-Parteikonferenz. Hamburg, C. Hoym Nachfolger, 1927. 63 p. *NN MH CtY CSt-H*
La situation extérieure et intérieure de l'U.S.S.R. Rapport fait à la XVe conference de parti du gouvernement de Moscou. Paris, Bureau d'Éditions de Diffusion et de Publicité, 1927. 59 p. *NN MH NjP InU*

Metz, Impr. Populaire de Lorraine, 1927. 62 p. *UL-H*
Paris, n. p., 1927. 62 p.

Also in:
Die internationale Lage und die innere Lage der Sowjetunion. In: *Internationale Presse-Korrespondenz,* VII, no. 11, 1927, pp. 201—213.
The International Situation and the Inner Situation in the Soviet Union. In: *Inprecor,* VII, no. 10, 1927.

763 О национально-освободительной войне, империализме, защите отечества и германских оппозиционерах. In: *Правда,* no. 48, Feb. 27, 1927, p. 2.

764 О старинных традициях и современном культурном строительстве. In: *Революция и Культура,* no. 1, Nov. 15, 1927, pp. 17–20.

765 Об итогах объединенного пленума ЦК и ЦКК ВКП(б). In: *Правда,* no. 186, Aug. 18, 1927, pp. 3–4.

A speech to a meeting of activists of the Leningrad section of the Russian Communist Party, delivered by Bukharin on August 11, 1927; not to be confused with the following item with the same title. In this report, Bukharin summarized the results of the July 29 — August 9 meeting of the CC and the CCC of the Party.

Other editions:

Об итогах объединенного пленума ЦК и ЦКК ВКК(б). Доклад на собрании партактива Ленинградской организации ВКП(б) 11 августа 1927 г. **Москва—Ленинград, Гос. изд., 1927. 62 р.**

Москва—Ленинград, Гос. изд., 1927. 62 р. *NN MH DLC RZIA BS*

Ленинград, n. p., 1927. 168 p.

Ленинград, n. p., 1927. 168 p.

Итоги объединенного пленума ЦК и ЦКК ВКП(б). **Харьков, Пролетарий, 1927. 68 р.**

Also in:

Über das Ergebnis des vereinigten Plenums des ZK und der ZKK der KPSU. In: *Internationale Presse-Korrespondenz,* VII, no. 87, 1927, pp. 1881-1885; no. 88, pp. 1918-1921; no. 89, pp. 1932-1937.

766 Об итогах объединенного пленума ЦК и ЦКК ВКП(б). In: *Правда,* no. 253, Nov. 4, 1927, pp. 5–7.

A report to a meeting of Leningrad party activists delivered by Bukharin on October 26, 1927, concerning the October 21-23 session of the CC and CCC of the Party; not to be confused with the preceding item. See nos. 767, 776, and 779.

767 Партия и оппозиция на пороге XV партсъезда. Доклад на собрании актива Ленинградской организации ВКП(б) 26 октября 1927. Москва–Ленинград, Гос. изд., 1927. 122 p. See no. 766, *Об итогах объединенного пленума ЦК . . .,* a report delivered to the same meeting; also nos. 776 and 779.

Other editions:

Москва—Ленинград, Гос. изд., 1927. 122 р.

Also in:

В защиту пролетарской диктатуры. Сборник. Москва—Ленинград Гос. изд., 1928. 260 р. *NN DLC BrM DS BS RZIA*

768 **Перспективы китайской революции.** In: *Революционный Восток,* no. 1, 1927, pp. 3—21.

A speech delivered to a meeting of students of the Communist University of Workers of the East, held in January 1927.

Also in:
Perspektiven der chinesischen Revolution. In: *Die Kommunistische Internationale,* VIII, no. 14, 1927, pp. 663—676.
The Position of the Chinese Revolution. In: *Inpretor,* VII, no. 39, 1927.

769 **[Platform submitted by Nikolai Bukharin, Yurii Piatakov, and Evgeniia Bosh . . .]** (1915). See no. 14.

770 **Празднование 10-летия Октябрьской революции. Торжественный пленум Московского совета. Речь тов. Н. И. Бухарина.** In: *Правда,* no. 257, Nov. 10, 1927, p. 3.

771 **Проблемы китайской революции.** Москва, «Правда» и «Беднота,» 1927. 62 p. *NjP RZIA*

Other editions:
Die Probleme der chinesischen Revolution. Hamburg—Berlin, C. Hoym Nachfolger, 1927. 63 p. *DS SB-N OFU-W*
Les problèmes de la révolution chinoise. Paris, Bureau d'Éditions de Diffusion et de Publicité, 1927. 61 p. *CSt-H ICU DS UL-H*
I problemi della rivoluzione cinese. Paris, n. p., 1927. 59 p.
Paris, n. p., 1930. 63 p.
Problems of the Chinese Revolution. Translated from the Russian by Eden and Cedar Paul. London, Communist Party of Great Britain, 1927. 50 p. *CLU*

Also in:
Вопросы китайской революции. Москва—Ленинград, Гос. изд., 1927 240 p. *NNC CSt-H*

772 **Путь к социализму и рабоче-крестьянский блок.** (1925). See no. 627.

773 **Речь тов. Н. И. Бухарина на президиуме ИККИ.** In: *Коммунистический Интернационал,* no. 41 (115), 1927, pp. 8—17.

774 **Речь тов. Н. И. Бухарина на торжественном заседании в Доме Союзов по поводу юбилея Клары Цеткин 5 июля 1927 г.** In: *Правда,* no. 151, July 7, 1927, p. 3.

775 **Речь тов. Н. И. Бухарина на похоронах тов. Рутенберга.** In: *Правда,* no. 94, Apr. 28, 1927, p. 3.

776 **Речи на октябрьском пленуме ЦК и ЦКК ВКП(б) по вопросу фракционной борьбы тт. Троцкого и Зиновьева после августовского пленума ЦК и ЦКК ВКП(б). Речь тов. Н. И. Бухарина.** In: *Правда,* no. 251, Nov. 2, 1927, p. 3. See nos. 766, 767, and 779.

777 **[Remarks of Bukharin.]** In: *XV съезд Всесоюзной Коммунистической партии (б). Стенографической отчет.* Москва–Ленинград Гос., изд., 1928. 1416 p.
Available in various libraries.

778 **The Russian Revolution and Social Democracy.** (1926). See no. 721.

779 **Schlusswort des Genossen Bucharin auf dem erweiterten Plenum des ZK und der ZKK der KPSU.** In: *Die Kommunistische Internationale,* VIII, no. 41, 1927, pp. 1988–2006.

Bukharin's concluding remarks at the October 21—23 session of the Central Committee and the Central Control Commission of the Russian Communist Party. See nos. 766, 767, and 776.

780 **Текущий момент китайской революции.** In: *Правда,* no. 145, June 30, 1927, p. 2.

Also in:
Вопросы китайской революции. Москва—Ленинград, Гос. изд., 1927. 240 p.
NNC CSt-H

781 **Textes choisis, recueillis par A. Bernard,** by Bukharin *et al.* N. p., n. p., 1927.

Contents and location of this item are unknown.

782 **La théorie du matérialisme historique . . .** (1921). See no. 377.

783 **[Theses on the national question submitted by N. Bukharin, Yurii Piatakov, and Evgeniia Bosh . . .]** (1915). See no. 17.

784 **The True Causes of the Resignation of the Cadets.** (1918).

A translation of part of *От диктатуры империализма к диктатуре пролетариата* . . . See no. 160.

785 **Великая борьба.** In: *Правда,* no. 97, May 1, 1927, p. 1.

786 **Владимир Ильич Ленин.** In: *Памяти погибших вождей.* Москва, n. p., 1927.

Contents and location of this item are unknown.

787 **Вопросы китайской революции.** Москва–Ленинград, Гос. изд., 1927. 240 p. *NNC CSt-H*

Contents. — Текущий момент китайской революции. — Проблемы китайской революции. — О китайской революции. Доклад Н. И. Бухарина на III плнуме МК ВКП(б).

See main entries for each of the first two titles; see *Итоги пленума ИККИ* (no. 745) for the third.

788 **За ленинизм,** by N. Bukharin and I. Stalin. N. p., n. p., 1927. See no. 731.

789 **Живой Ленин.** In: *Правда,* no. 91, Apr. 22, 1927, p. 1.

790 **Злые заметки.** In: *Правда,* no. 9, Jan. 12, 1927, p. 2.

Other editions:
Злые заметки. Москва, Гос. изд., 1927. 19 p. *NN*

Also in:
Этюды. Москва—Ленинград, Государственное технико-теоретическое изд., 1932. *NN NNC ICU BS*

1928

791 **Чего хотим мы от Горького?** In: *Правда,* no. 75, Mar. 29, 1928, p. 2.

Also in:
Народное просвещение, no. 4, 1928.

792 **Le communisme et la question nationale et coloniale . . .** (1927). See no. 734.

793 **Comrade Bukharin on the Forged "Bukharin Letter."** In: *Inprecor,* VIII, no. 17, 1928. See no. 818.

794 **Comrade Bukharin's Speech in Reply to the Debate on the Programme Question.** In: *Inprecor,* VII, no. 59, 1928.

See the verbatim records of the Sixth World Congress of the Comintern (no. 826) for a full account of Bukharin's remarks.

795 **l'Economie mondiale . . .** (1917). See no. 82.

796 **Экономика и классы.** N. p., n. p., 1928.

797 **Die Ergebnisse des 6. Weltkongresses der Kommunistischen Internationale. Auf dem 5. Kongress der Kommunistischen Jugendinternationale.** In: *Internationale Presse-Korrespondenz,* VIII, no. 121, 1928, pp. 2367–2402. See no. 803.

798 **Der Februar-Umsturz.** In: *Illustrierte Geschichte der russischen Revolution 1917.* Herausgegeben von W. Astrow, A. Slepkow, J. Thomas. Berlin, n. p., 1928. *OFU-G*

Other editions:
An Illustrated History of the Russian Revolution. London, n. p., 1928. 2 vols.

799 **Historical Materialism . . .** (1921). See no. 377.

800 **Империализм и накопление капитала . . .** (1924). See no. 477.

801 **The International Position and the Tasks of the Communist International.** (1927). See no. 757.

802 **Die internationale Lage und die Aufgaben der Kommunistischen Internationale . . .** (1927). See no. 757.

803 **Итоги VI конгресса Коммунистического Интернационала. Доклад тов. Н. И. Бухарина на собрании актива Московской организации ВКП(б).** In: *Правда,* no. 212, Sept. 12, 1928, pp. 3–4. See no. 797.

Other editions:

Итоги VI конгресса Коммунистического Интернационала. Доклад на собрании актива Московской организации ВКП(б) 5 сентября 1928 года. Москва, Гос. изд., 1928. 58 p.
Москва, Гос. изд., 1928. 58 p. *DLC*
Москва—Ленинград, n. p., 1928. 58 p. *DLC RZIA*

Die historische Leistung des 6. Weltkongresses der Komintern. Rede vor dem Parteiaktiv der Moskauer Organisation der KPdSU, 5. September 1928. Hamburg, C. Hoym Nachfolger, 1928? 34 p. *NN MH CtY DS OFU-W BHW CSt-H*

Ergebnisse des VI. Kongresses der Kommunistischen Internationale. Rede, gehalten vor dem Parteiaktiv der Moskauer Organisation der KP(B)SU. Anschliessend J. Jaroslawski: Über die KP(B)SU und die Opposition auf dem 6. Kominternkongress (mit Wort-Erklärung). Moskau, Zentral-Völker-Verlag, 1929. 66 p. *NN DS BS*

Also in:

Ergebnisse des 6. Kongresses der Kommunistischen Internationale. In: *Internationale Presse-Korrespondenz,* VIII, no. 108, 1928, pp. 2059—2070.

The Results of the Sixth World Congress of the C. I. In: *Inprecor,* VIII, no. 70, 1928.

804 **Из речей Н. К. Крупской, Н. И. Бухарина, А. Б. Луначарского и Н. А. Семашка по основным вопросам педагогики.** In: *На путях к новой школе,* no. 1, Jan. 1928, pp. 9–14.

805 **К вопросу о закономерностях переходного периода...** (1926). See no. 681.

806 **Ленинизм и проблема культурной революции.** In: *Правда,* no. 23, Jan. 27, 1928, pp. 5–6.

Other editions:

Ленинизм и проблема культурной революции. Речь на траурном заседании памяти В. И. Ленина. Москва—Ленинград, Гос. изд., 1928. 46 p. *WB RZIA*

Also in:

Известия, no. 23, Jan. 27, 1928, pp. 3—4.

Народное просвещение, no. 2, 1928, pp. 3—20.

Народный учитель, no. 1/2, 1928, pp. 78—92.

Der Leninismus und das Problem der Kulturrevolution. In: *Internationale Presse-Korrespondenz,* VIII, no. 12, 1928, pp. 238-241; no. 13, pp. 263-265; no. 14, pp. 285-287.

Leninism and the Problem of Cultural Revolution. In: *Inprecor,* VIII, no. 6, 1928, p. 158; no. 8, p. 183; no. 9, p. 209.

807 **Международная буржуазия и Карл Каутский — ее апостол.** (1925). In: *В защиту пролетарской диктатуры.* See no. 834; also no. 598.

808 Международное положение и задачи Коминтерна. Отчетный доклад исполкома Коминтерна и заключительное слово на VI конгрессе Коминтерна. Москва, Гос. изд., 1928. 174 p.

NNC DLC CSt-H CtY DS BS

For the complete record of Bukharin's remarks to the Sixth Congress of the Comintern, see no. 826.

Other editions:
Москва—Ленинград, n. p., 1928. 174 p.
Международное положение и задачи Коминтерна. Отчет исполкома Коммунистического Интернационала. Доклад тов. Н. И. Бухарина. Архангельск, n. p., 1928. 48 p.

Also in:
Die internationale Lage und die Aufgaben der Komintern. In: *Internationale Presse-Korrespondenz,* VIII, 1928.

809 На темы дня. In: *Правда,* no. 122, May 27, 1928, p. 2.

810 Наука и СССР. (1927). See no. 760.

811 Наука и технка за десять лет. (1927—1928). See no. 760.

812 Die neuesten Erscheinungen der Stabilisierung des Kapitalismus . . . (1927). See no. 761.

813 О характеристике нашей революции и о возможности победоносного социалистического строительства в СССР. (1926). In: *В защиту пролетарской диктатуры.* See no. 834, also no. 695.

814 О Кольцове. In: *Михаил Кольцов. Статьи и материалы,* by Bukharin *et al.* Ленинград, Академия, 1928. 126 p. *CU*

815 О некоторых вопросах из первой части проекта программы К. И. Из речи тов. Н. И. Бухарина в программной комиссии. In: *Коммунистический Интернационал,* no. 31/32 (157/158), April, 1928, pp. 32—40.

Other editions:
Über einige Fragen des ersten Teiles des Programm-Entwurfes der KI. Aus einer Rede des Genossen Bucharin in der Programmkommission. In: *Die Kommunistische Internationale,* IX, no. 33/34, 1928, pp. 2059-2069.

816 О текущих задачах комсомола. In: *Правда,* no. 110, May 13, 1928, pp. 3–4.

Bukharin's report to the Eighth Congress of the Komsomol. For a complete record of his remarks, see no. 827.

Other editions:
Текущие задачи комсомола. Доклад на VIII всесоюзном съезде ВЛКСМ 6 мая 1928 г. Москва, n. p., 1928. 56 p.
Москва, n. p., 1928. 56 p.

817 Очередные задачи партии . . . (1927). See no. 731.

818 Опровержение, которое было бы излишне, если бы на свете было меньше дураков. In: *Правда,* no. 57, Mar. 7, 1928, p. 2.

In this article Bukharin repudiated his alleged authorship of the letter attributed to him in "Brothers in Lenin." See no. 571; see also no. 793.

819 Отчет делегации ВКП(б) в ИККИ XV съезду ВКП(б) . . . (1927). See no. 757.

820 Партия и оппозиция на пороге XV съезда партии. (1927). In: *В защиту пролетарской диктатуры.* See no. 834; also no. 767.

821 Пленум исполкома Коминтерна. Об оппозиции в ВКП(б) и в Коминтерне. Доклад тов. Н. И. Бухарина. In: *Правда,* no. 41, Feb. 7, 1928, p. 2.

Also in:
Die Opposition in der KPSU und in der Komintern. Diskussion. In: *Internationale Presse-Korrespondenz,* VIII, no. 18, 1928, pp. 369—390.
Ninth Plenum of the ECCI; Full Report; The Opposition in the CPSU and in the Comintern; Report of Comrade Bukharin. In: *Inprecor,* VIII, no. 10, 1928.

822 Празднование 11-й годовщины Октября . . . речь тов. Н. И. Бухарина. In: *Правда,* no. 261, Nov. 10, 1928, p. 3.

823 Профессор с пикой. In: *Правда,* no. 249, Oct. 25, 1928, p. 3.

This article commemorated the 60th birthday of M. N. Pokrovsky.

824 Программа Коммунистического Интернационала.

Although the authorship of the 1928 Program of the Communist International was at the time of its adoption and still is officially attributed to the drafting committee that reported it out to the Sixth Congress of the Comintern, recent research substantiates the heretofore unconfirmed belief that Bukharin was its actual author. It was published shortly after adoption and subsequently reissued in every major language and in numerous editions, and it is available in various libraries. The editions, translations, and versions of this program are so numerous and so widely distributed that no effort is made here to list them. See nos. 236, 398, and 525 for earlier versions of the program that Bukharin submitted in 1928.

825 Программный вопрос на VI конгрессе Коммунистического Интернационала. Доклад и заключительное слово. Москва—Ленинград, n. p., 1928. 94 p. *DS*

For a complete record of Bukharin's remarks at the Sixth Congress of the Comintern, see no. 826.

826 [Remarks of Bukharin.] In: *VI конгресс Коминтерна. Стенографический отчет.* Москва, Гос., изд., 1929. 6 vols.

Available in various libraries and in translation.

827 [Remarks of Bukharin.] In: *VIII Всесоюзный съезд ВЛКСМ. Стенографический отчет.* Москва, Молодая гвардия, 1928. 602 p. *NN DLC*

828 [Report of Bukharin, Международное положение и задачи Коммунистического Интернационала.] (1927). See no. 757.

829 La situation internationale et les tâches de l'I. C. . . . (1927). See no. 757.

830 Текущий момент и задачи нашей печати. In: *Правда,* no. 280, Dec. 2, 1928, pp. 3–4.

Other editions:

Текущий момент и задачи нашей печати. Доклад на 41-м совещании рабселькоров. Иошкар-Ола, Маробиздата, 1928. 26 p.

831 Теория исторического материализма... (1921). See no. 377.

832 Цезаризм под маской революции. (1925). In: *В защиту пролетарской диктатуры.* See no. 834; also no. 646.

833 Уроки хлебозаготовок, шахтинского дела и задачи партии. К итогам апрельского пленума ЦК ВКП(б). In: *Правда,* no. 91, Apr. 19, 1928, pp. 3–4.

Other editions:

Уроки хлебозаготовок, шахтинского дела и задачи партии. К итогам апрельского пленума ЦК и ЦКК ВКП(б). Доклад на собрании актива Ленинградской организации ВКП(б) 13 апреля 1928 г. Ленинград, Прибой, 1928. 93 p. *NNC RZIA*

Ленинград, n. p., 1928. 93 p.

Also in:

Die Lehren der Getreidebeschaffungskampagne, die Ereignisse von Schachty und die Aufgaben der KPSU. In *Internationale Presse-Korrespondenz,* VIII, no. 41, 1928, pp. 734—737; no. 42, pp. 755—758; no. 43, pp. 771—774.

834 В защиту пролетарской диктатуры. Сборник. Москва–Ленинград, Гос. изд., 1928. 260 p. *NN DLC BrM DS BS RZIA*

Contents. — Партия и оппозиция на пороге XV съезда партии (1927). — О характере нашей революции и о возможности победоносного социалистического строительства в СССР (1926). — Цезаризм под маской революции (1925). — Международная буржуазия и Карл Каутский — ее апостол (1925). See also the main entries for each of these items under the year of original publication indicated.

835 Världslägets problem; socialdemokratiens eller kommunismens väg? En koncentrerad analys nyåret 1928. Stockholm, Frams Vörlag, 1928. 54 p. *MH*

836 Вопросы культуры и культурного строительства на XV съезде ВКП(б). In: *Народный учитель,* no. 3/4, 1928, pp. 36–50.

837 Всемирный конгресс друзей СССР. N. p., n. p., 1928.

838 Заметки экономиста (К началу нового хозяйственного года). In: *Правда,* no. 228, Sept. 30, 1928, pp. 2–3.

This article was one of Bukharin's last relatively free public criticisms of Stalin's policies concerning the rate and methods of industrialization and collectivization leading to the inauguration of the First Five Year Plan, in which he reasserted his belief in the necessity for and the efficacy of the gradualist approach to socialism in the USSR.

Other editions:
Заметки экономиста. К началу нового хозяйственного года. Москва—Ленинград, Гос. изд., 1928. 56 p. *DLC*

Also in:
Vor dem elften Jahrestag der Oktoberrevolution. Zum Beginn des neuen Wirtschaftsjahres in der Sowjetunion. In: *Internationale Presse-Korrespondenz,* VIII, no. 117, 1928, pp. 2291—2295; no. 118, pp. 2320—2322; no. 19, pp. 2340—2342.
Before the 11th Anniversary of the October Revolution. In: *Inprecor,* VIII, nos. 70, 73, 75, 1928.

839 Заветы Ленина и рабкоры. (1924). See no. 560.

1929

840 Ergebnisse des VI. Kongresses der Kommunistischen Internationale . . . (1928). See no. 803.

841 [Финансовый капитал в мантии папы. Памфлет.]

This pamphlet, a classic of vitriolic polemic, was written in 1929. The earliest extant edition is a French version, the language in which it was perhaps first published. The earliest available Russian version is in *Правда,* but it was not published until March 1930. The fact that it first appeared in Russian in 1930, after the 1929 French edition, would indicate that French was the first language of publication and its appearance in *Правда* would indicate that this newspaper version preceded the independent Russian edition.

Other editions:
Le Pape contre l'Union Soviétique. Ce que dissimule le manteau sanglant et hypocrite du Pontife de Rome. Paris, Impr. Centrale, 1929. 24 p. *UL-H*
Финансовый капитал в мантии папы (Памфлет). In: *Правда,* no. 65, Mar. 7, 1930, pp. 2—4.
Финансовый капитал в мантии папы. Памфлет. Москва, Безбожник, 1930. 32 p. *RZIA*
Das Finanzkapital im päpstlichen Hermelin. Pamphlet. Moskau, n. p., 1930. 31 p.
Moskau, n. p., 1930. 32 p.
Charkow, n. p., 1930. 32 p.
Minsk, n. p., 1930. 32 p.

Warum päpstlicher Kreuzzug gegen die Sowjetunion? Ein Pamphlet. Hamburg-Berlin, n. p., 1930. 24 p. *UFU*
Réponse au Pape. Pamphlet. N. p., n. p., 1930.
Kapitał finansowy w płaszczu papieskim. Pamflet. Przekład H. Domskiego. Moskwa, n. p., 1930. 50 p.
Charków, n. p., 1930. 50 p.
Minsk, n. p., 1930. 50 p.
Finanza kapitalo en la Papa mantelo. Pamfleto. Moskvo, n. p., 1930. 32 p.
Finanze Capital in Papal Robes. A Challenge. Trans. by Moissaye J. Olgin. New York, Friends of the Soviet Union, 1930 ? 23 p. *NN NNC MH CLU*

Also in:
Этюды. Москва—Ленинград, Государственное технико-теоретическое изд., 1932. 352 p. *NN NNC ICU BS*
Finance Capital in Papal Robes. A Challenge. In: *Inprecor,* X, no. 14, 1930.

842 Imperialism and World Economy. (1917). See no. 82.

843 Imperialismus und Weltwirtschaft. (1917). See no. 82.

844 Империализм и накопление капитала . . . (1924). See no. 477.

845 [Introduction to] A. Aikhenval'd, Советская экономика. (1927). Москва—Ленинград, Гос. изд., 1929. 372 p. *NN BDIC*

The introduction to this book was written in 1927 but not published until 1929.

846 [Introduction to] Mikhail Kol'tsov, Собрание сочинений. Москва—Ленинград, n. p., 1929. 442 p.

847 [К постановке проблем теории исторического материализма (Беглые заметки).] (1923). In: *Теория исторического материализма . . .* See no. 420.

848 Ленин и задачи науки в социалистическом строительстве. In: *Правда,* no. 17, Jan. 20, 1929, pp. 2–3.

849 Надежда Константиновна (К шестидесятилетию тов. Крупской). In: *Правда,* no. 48, Feb. 27, 1929, p. 3.

850 Некоторые проблемы современного капитализма у теоретиков буржуазии. In: *Правда,* no. 118, May 26, 1929, pp. 2–3.

This article, together with his article, Теория «организованной бесхозяйственности,» published in the same year (see no. 857), was Bukharin's most extreme and developed expression of his theory of "organized capitalism," first advanced in 1916 in his *К теории империалистического государства* (see no. 25) and in 1917 in his *Мировое хозяйство и империализм* (see no. 82). It also received further expression in 1924 in his *Империализм и накопление капитала* (see no. 477). In 1929 the *Правда* articles became the subject of a critical discussion in the Institute of World Economy and World Politics of the Communist Academy with the intent of discrediting Bukharin as part of the campaign against him launched in that year by Stalin.

Also in:
«Организованный капитализм.» Дискуссия в Комакадемии. 2 изд. [Москва(?)], Коммунистическая Академия, 1930. 200 p. *CSt-H*

851 Le Pape contre l'Union Soviétique . . . See no. 841.

852 Политическое завещание Ленина. Доклад на траурном заседании, посвященном пятилетию со дня смерти Ленина. In: *Правда,* no. 19, Jan. 24, 1929, p. 2.

This speech was one of Bukharin's last public attacks against Stalin's seizure of power within the Party in late 1928, which took the form of an interpretation of Leninism, intended actually as a defense of Bukharin's own economic and political policies in the late 1920's.

Other editions:
Политическое завещание Ленина. Москва, «Правда» и «Беднота,» 1929. 31 p.
Москва, «Правда» и «Беднота,» 1929. 31 p. *CSt-H DLC MH WB RZIA*
Москва, n. p., 1929. 31 p.

Also in:
Политическое завещание Ленина. In: *Известия,* no. 19, Jan. 24, 1929, p. 2.

853 Программа Октября. К десятилетию программы нашей партии. In: *Правда,* no. 67, Mar. 23, 1929, pp. 2–3.

Other editions:
Программа Октября (К десятилетию программы нашей партии). Москва, «Правда» и «Беднота,» 1929. 16 p. *RZIA*

854 **Реконструкционный период и борьба с религией.** In: *Революция и Культура,* no. 12, June 30, 1929, pp. 3–13.

Other editions:
Реконструктивный период и борьба с религией. Доклад на 2-м всесоюзном съезде Союза безбожников. Москва, «Безбожник,» 1929. 31 p.

855 **Технико-экономическая революция, рабочий класс и инженерство.** In: *Правда,* no. 295, Dec. 15, 1929, p. 3.

856 **Теория исторического материализма . . .** (1921). See no. 377.

857 **Теория «организованной бесхозяйственности.»** In: *Правда,* no. 147. June 30, 1929, pp. 3–5.

See annotation for no. 850.

Also in:
«Организованный капитализм.» Дискуссия в Комакадемии. 2 изд. [Москва(?)], Коммунистическая академия, 1930. 200 p. *CSt-H*

858 **Заявление тт. Томского, Бухарина и Рыкова в ЦК ВКП(б).** In: *Правда,* no. 276, Nov. 26, 1929, p. 2.

1930

859 **La Delegazione Operaia Italiana in Russia. Le Questioni Russe nel Colloquio con Bucarin,** by Bukharin and [?] Losovskii. Paris, n. p., 1930. 64 p.

860 **La economía mundial . . .** (1917). See no. 82.

861 **The Economic Theory of the Leisure Class.** (1919). See no. 239.

862 **Financa kapitalo en la Papa mantelo . . .** (1929). See no. 841.

863 **Finance Capital in Papal Robes . . .** (1929). See no. 841.

864 Финансовый капитал в мантии папы. (1929). See no. 841.

865 Das Finanzkapital im päpstlichen Hermelin . . . (1929). See no. 841.

866 Imperialism and World Economy. (1917). See no. 82.

867 Kapitał finansowy w płaszczu papieskim . . . (1929). See no. 841.

868 На боевом посту. Сборник к шестидесятилетию Д. Б. Рязанова, by Bukharin *et al.* Москва, n. p., 1930.

Contents and location of this item are unknown.

869 Некоторые проблемы современного капитализма у теоретиков буржуазии. (1929). See no. 850.

870 I problemi della rivoluzione cinese. (1927). See no. 771.

871 Réponse au Pape . . . (1929). See no. 841.

872 Социалистическая реконструкция и естественные науки. In: *Этюды.* Москва–Ленинград, Государственное технико-теоретическое изд., 1932. 352 p. *NN NNC ICU BS*

A footnote to this article states that it was published independently in 1930, but there is no known record of this publication.

872a Теория «организованной бесхозяйственности». (1929). See no. 857.

873 Тезисы Н. И. Бухарина, предложенные им на Бернской конференции . . . (1915). See no. 16.

874 Warum päpstlicher Kreuzug gegen die Sowjetunion . . . (1929). See no. 841.

1931

875 Борьба двух миров и задачи науки. Москва, n. p., 1931. 31 p.

A report to the Extraordinary Session of the Academy of Sciences of the USSR held on June 21—27, 1931.

Other editions:
Москва—Ленинград, n. p., 1931. 31 p.

Der Kampf zweier Welten und die Aufgaben der Wissenschaft. Die Wissenschaft der UdSSR an einem weltgeschichtlichen Wendpunkt. Referat auf der ausserordentlichen Tagung der Akademie der Wissenschaften der UdSSR, Moskau 21—27 Juni 1931. Moskau, n. p., 1931. 36 p. *DS BS*

Also in:
Этюды. Москва—Ленинград, Государственное технико-теоретическое изд., 1932. 352 p. *NN NNC ICU BS*

876 Гейне и коммунизм. In: *Этюды.* Москва—Ленинград, Государственное технико-теоретическое изд., 1932. 352 p. *NN NNC ICU BS*

A report delivered to the Academy of Sciences of the USSR on April 29, 1931, and published in 1932.

877 Комсомольская начальная политшкола. Дополнительная беседа для комсомольцев шерстяной пром-сти, составлена тт. Бухариным и Косичкиным, by Bukharin and [?] Kosichkin. Москва, n. p., 1931. 28 p.

Contents and location of this item are unknown.

878 О технической пропаганде и ее организации. Москва—Ленинград, Красный пролетарий, 1931. 48 p. *NN NNC*

A report to a group of industrial and economic administrators delivered on August 26, 1931.

Other editions:
Москва, n. p., 1931. 72 p.

Die sozialistische Rekonstruktion und der Kampf um die Technik; Über die technische Propaganda und ihre Organisation. Moskau, n. p., 1931. 36 p. *DS*

Socialist Reconstruction and the Struggle for Technique. Moscow, Co-operative Publishing Society of Foreign Workers in the USSR, 1932. 32 p. *NN NNC CSt-H CtY ICU CU CLU WaU OFU-W*

Also in:
Социалистическая реконструкция и борьба за технику. О технической пропаганде и ее организации. In: *Этюды.* Москва—Ленинград, Государственное технико-теоретическое изд., 1932. 352 p. *NN NNC ICU BS*

879 Основы планирования научно-исследовательской работы. Москва —Ленинград, Государственное социально-экономическое изд., 1931. 71 p. *ICU*

A report to the first all-union conference on planning of scientific research, held in 1931.

Other editions:
Москва—Ленинград, Красный пролетарий, 1931. 72 p.

Also in:
Этюды Москва—Ленинград, Государственное технико-теоретическое изд., 1932. 352 p. *NN NNC ICU BS*

880 Science and Politics in the Soviet Union. In: *New Statesman and Nation,* Nov. 7, 1931, pp. 37–38.

881 Школа, общественность, техническая пропаганда. Речь на Всероссийской конференции по производительному обучению ФЗС. Москва, Народный комиссариат просвещения, 1931. 16 p.

882 Theory and Practice from the Standpoint of Dialectical Materialism. London, Kniga, 1931. 23 p. *NNC CLU*

On the cover: "Science at the Crossroads; Papers Read to the Second International Congress of the History of Science and Technology, by the Delegates of the U.S.S.R. London, June 29th to July 3rd, 1931."

Other editions:
Теория и практика с точки зрения диалектического материализма. Москва—Ленинград, n. p., 1932. 32 p.

Also in:
Этюды. Москва—Ленинград, Государственное технико-теоретическое изд., 1932. 352 p. *NN NNC ICU BS*

1932

883 Борьба двух миров и задачи науки. (1931). In: *Этюды.* See no. 885; also no. 875.

884 **Дарвинизм и марксизм. Доклад на торжественном заседании, посвященном пятидесятилетию со дня смерти Чарлса Дарвина.** Ленинград, Изд. Академии наук, 1932. 35 p.

Other editions:
Ленинград, Изд., Академии наук, 1932. 35 p. *NN NNC*

Also in:
Этюды. See no. 885.

885 **Этюды.** Москва–Ленинград, Государственное технико-теоретическое изд., 1932. 352 p. *NN NNC ICU BS*

Contents. — Социалистическая реконструкция и естественные науки (1930). — Социалистическая реконструкция и борьба за технику... (1931). — Теория и практика с точки зрения диалектического материализма (1931). — Борьба двух миров и задачи науки (1931). — Дарвинизм и марксизм (1932). — Гете и его историческое значение (1932). — Гейне и коммунизм (1931). — Валерий Брюсов и Владимир Маяковский (1932). — Основы планирования научно-исследовательской работы (1931). — Злые заметки (1927). — Техника и экономика современного капитализма (1932). — Финансовый капитал в мантии папы (1929).

886 **Финансовый капитал в мантии папы.** (1929). In: *Этюды.* See no. 885; also no. 841.

887 **Гейне и коммунизм.** (1931). In: *Этюды.* See no. 885; also no. 876.

888 **Гете и его историческое значение. Речь, прочитанная на торжественном заседании Академии наук СССР, посвященном 100-летию со дня смерти Гете.** Ленинград, Изд. Академии наук СССР, 1932. 39 p.

DLC NS-U

Also in:
Этюды. See no. 885.

889 **Der Imperialismus und die Akkumulation des Kapitals.** (1924). See no. 477.

890 **[Letters exchanged between Bukharin and Lenin concerning their dispute . . .]** (1916). In: Из материалов Института Маркса-Энгельса-Ленина . . . See no. 26.

891 **Основы планирования научно-исследовательской работы.** (1931). In: *Этюды.* See no. 885; also no. 879.

892 **Памяти М. Н. Покровского. Речь т. Н. И. Бухарина на траурном митинге, посвященном памяти М. Н. Покровского.** In: *Вестник Коммунистической академии,* no. 4/5, April–May, 1932, pp. 8–11.

This meeting was held on April 13, 1932.

893 **Die politische Ökonomie des Rentners . . .** (1919). See no. 239.

894 **[Remarks of Bukharin.]** In: *XVII конференция Всесоюзной Коммунистической партии (б). Стенографический отчет.* Москва, Партийное изд., 1932. 296 p. *Available in various libraries.*

895 **Socialist Reconstruction and the Struggle for Technique.** (1931). See no. 878.

896 **Социалистическая реконструкция и борьба за технику.** (1931). In: *Этюды.* See no. 885; also no. 878.

897 **Социалистическая реконструкция и естественные науки.** (1930). In: *Этюды.* See no. 885; also no. 872.

898 **The Soviets Plan Science.** Trans. by Andrew Rothstein. London, Williams and Norgate, 1932.

899 **Техническая реконструкция и текущие проблемы научно-исследовательской работы. Доклад на 2-й Всесоюзной конференции по планированию научно-исследовательской работы в тяжелой промышленности.** Москва, n. p., 1932. 40 p.

900 **Техника и экономика современного капитализма. Речь на торжественном годовом собрании Академии наук СССР, 29 февраля 1932 г.** Ленинград, Изд. Академии наук СССР, 1932. 36 p.
NN NNC MH DS

Other editions:
Ленинград, Изд. Академии наук СССР, 1932. 36 p.

Also in:
Этюды. See no. 885.

901 **Теория и практика с точки зрения диалектического материализма.** (1931). In: *Этюды.* See no. 885; also no. 882.

902 **Валерий Брюсов и Владимир Маяковский.** In: *Этюды.* See no. 885.

903 **Елые заметки.** (1927). In: *Этюды.* See no. 885; also no. 790.

1933

904 **Historical Materialism . . .** (1921). See no. 377.

905 **El Materialismo Historico . . .** (1921). See no. 377.

906 **Платформа Коммунистического Интернационала . . .** (1919). In: *Коммунистический Интернационал в документах . . .* See no. 236.

907 **Речь тов. Н. И. Бухарина на объединенном пленуме ЦК и ЦКК ВКП(б).** In: *Правда,* no. 14, Jan. 14, 1933, p. 3.

This speech contains one of Bukharin's public recantations following his fall from power in 1929.

Also in:
Известия, no. 14, Jan. 14, 1933, p. 3.

908 **Учение Маркса и его историческое значение.** N. p., Изд. Академии Наук СССР, 1933. 99 p. *DLC*

Also in:
Marx's Teaching and Its Historical Importance. In: *Marxism and Modern Thought,* by N. I. Bukharin, A. M. Deborin, *et al.;* trans. by Ralph Fox. London, G. Routledge, and New York, Harcourt Brace, 1935. 342 p.
NN NNC MH DLC ICU CtY NjP CSt-H CU OCL InU CLU IU WaU BrM

1934

909 **Historical Materialism . . .** (1921). See no. 377.

910 **[Introduction to] D. V. and M. I. Radovskii, Динамовщина ее историческом развитии. Документы и материалы.** Ленинград, n. p., 1934. 560 p.

911 **[Introduction to] Valentin F. Asmus, Маркс, Энгельс, Ленин, Сталин о технике. Сборник материалов с предисловием Н. И. Бухарина. Составил В. Ф. Асмус.** Москва, Гос. технико-теоретическое изд., 1934. 635 p. *NN*

912 **Кризис капиталистической культуры и проблемы культуры в СССР.** In: *Известия,* no. 56, Mar. 6, 1934, p. 4; no. 66, Mar. 18, 1934, p. 5.

Other editions:
Culture in Two Worlds; The Crisis of Capitalist Culture and the Problems of Culture in the U.S.S.R. New York, International Pamphlets, 1934. 31 p.
NN NNC MH CU CLU CSt-H CtY IU ICU WaU

913 **Почему мы побеждаем?** In: *Известия,* no. 102, May 1, 1934, p. 3.

Also in:
Why We Shall Be Victorious. In: *Inprecor,* XIV, no. 30, 1934.

914 **Поэзия, поэтика и задачи поэтического творчества в СССР.** Москва, Гос. изд. художественной литературы, 1934, 51 p.
NN NNC

Other editions:

Поэзия, поэтика и задачи поэтического творчества в СССР. Доклад и заключительное слово на первом всесоюзном съезде советских писателей. Москва, Гос. изд. «Художественная литература,» 1934. 95 p. *NN MH CU*

Also in:

Poetry, Poetics, and the Problems of Poetry in the U.S.S.R. In: *Problems of Soviet Literature. Reports and Speeches at the First Soviet Writers' Congress,* by A. Zhdanov, Maxim Gorky, N. Bukharin, K. Radek, A. Stetsky. New York, International Publishers, 1935. 278 p. *NN NNC CtY IU ICU OCl InU*

Poetry, the Theory of Poetry, and the Tasks of Poetic Creation in the Soviet Union. In: *Inprecor,* XIV, no. 50, 1934.

Runous, Runouden Teoria ja Tehtävät Luomistyössä Runouden alalla Neuvostoliitossa. In: *Neuvostokirjailijain Yleisliittolainen Edustajakokous; Selostukset ja Päätökset; Toimittaanut Jalmari Virtanen.* Petrozavodsk, n. p., 1935, pp. 191—265.

915 **[Remarks of Bukharin.]** In: *XVII съезд Всесоюзной коммунистической Партии (б). Стенографический отчет.* Москва, Партийное издательство, 1934. 716 p.
Available in various libraries.

1935

916 **Человек творец.** In: *Иван Владимирович Мичурин. Его замечательная жизнь и работа, 1855—1935. Сборник статей.* Воронеж, n. p., 1935. 86 p.

917 **[Introduction to] C. Darwin, X. Дарвин, Происхождение видов. Пер. А. Тимирязева. С исправлениями и указателями под общ. ред. Н. И. Вавилова. Вводные статьи Н. И. Бухарина и Н. И. Вавилова.** Москва—Ленинград, Сельхозгиз, 1935, 630 p. *NN*

918 **Marx's Teaching and Its Historical Importance.** (1933). See no. 908.

919 **An Outstanding Man, an Untiring Revolutionary.** In: *Inprecor,* XV, no. 18. 1935.

920 **Poetry, Poetics, and the Problems of Poetry in the USSR.** (1934). In: *Problems of Soviet Literature* ... See no. 914.

921 **Runous, runouden teoria ja tehtävät luomistyössä runouden ...** (1934). See no. 914.

922 **Some Results of the Revolutionary Year – and Our Enemies.** In: *Inprecor,* XV, no. 63, 1935.

923 **Жизнь для революции.** In: N. V. Krylenko, *Задачи органов юстиции. С приложением статьи Н. И. Бухарина к 50-летию Н. В. Крыленко «Жизнь для революции».* Москва, Совет законодальства, 1935. 31 p. *BDIC*

1936

924 **Imperialism and Communism.** In: *Foreign Affairs,* XIV, no. 4, July, 1936, pp. 563–577.

925 **[Introduction to] B. L. Bogaevskii, История техники. Том 1, Часть 1: Техника первобытно-коммунистического общества.** Москва, Академия наук, 1936. 635 p. *BiN UL-H*

926 **[Introduction to] Iakov V. Apushkin, Константин Федорович Юон.** Москва, Всехудожник, 1936. 113 p. *NNC UL-H*

927 **Михаил Иванович Калинин. К 60-летию со дня рождения.** Москва, Институт красных профессоров, 1936. 24 p. *BDIC*

928 **Нужна-ли нам марксистская историческая наука.** In: *Известия,* no. 23, Jan. 27, 1936, pp. 3–4.

Also in:
На фронте исторической науки. N. p., n. p., 19—?, pp. 85—103.

929 Les problèmes fondamentaux de la culture contemporaine. Paris, Association pour l'Étude de la Culture Soviétique, 1936. 32 p.

BDIC CSt-H

One of Bukharin's last publications before his trial and execution in 1938. It is a speech delivered on April 3, 1936, to a conference of the Association for the Study of Soviet Culture in Paris. It was published originally in French and was never translated into or published in Russian.

1937

930 El programa militar... (1919). See no. 194.

1938

931 El materialismo historico... (1921). See no. 377.

932 [Remarks of Bukharin as defendant.] In: *Судебный отчет по делу антисоветского »право-троцкистского блока«, рассмотренному Военной коллегией Верховного Суда Союза ССР 2—13 марта 1938 г. по обвинению Бухарина, Н. И., Рыкова...* Москва, Юридическое издат. НКЮ СССР, 1938. 383 p.

Available in various libraries.

Other editions:

Report of Court Proceedings in the Case of the Anti-Soviet "Bloc of Rights and Trotskyites"... Moscow, The People's Commissariat of Justice of the U.S.S.R., 1938. 799 p. *Many libraries*

Prozessbericht über die Strafsache des antisowjetischen "Blocks der Rechten und Trotzkisten"... Moskau, Hrsg. vom Volkskommissariat für Justizwesen der UdSSR, 1938. 871 p. *InU*

Le procès du "Bloc des droitiers et des Trotskistes antisoviétique"... Moscou, Le Commissariat du Peuple de la Justice de l'U.R.S.S., 1938. 849 p. *NjP InU CLU*

Rättengangen mot "Högerns och Trotskisternas Block"... Stockholm, Arbetarkultur, 1938. *MH*

Il processo del "Blocco Antisovietico dei Destri e dei Trotskisti"... Parigi, Edicioni di Coltura Sociale, 1938. 138 p. *CSt-H*

1952

933 **Kyōsan Shugi no ABC...** (1919). See no. 194.

1954

934 **El A B C del comunismo.** (1919). See no. 194.

1963

935 **ABC du communisme...** (1919). See no. 194.

DATE UNKNOWN

936 **Что делало его великим?** In: *Известия,* Казань, no. 21, 19–?

937 **Что делало Ленина выразителем миллионов?** In: *Ленинцы,* no. 1, 19–?, p. 30.

INDEX

Numerals following titles refer to entry numbers. Titles beginning with a numerical digit are listed separately in numerical order at the beginning of the alphabetical listing.

INDEX

A (A)

B (Б)

C (Ч)

D (Д)

E (Е, Ё, Э)

F (Ф)

G (Г)

H

I (И, Я, Ю)

J

K (К, X)

L (Л)

M (M)

N (H)

О (О)

P (П)

Q

R (P)

S (С, Ш, Щ)

Т (T, Ц)

U (У)

V (B)

W

Y

Z (З, Ж)